Huntington v. Aster

HUNTINGTON V. ASTER

Warren A. Jones
and
Joseph E. Taylor

Professors of Law
Pacific McGeorge School of Law
University of the Pacific
Sacramento, California

NITA®
NATIONAL INSTITUTE FOR TRIAL ADVOCACY

Address inquiries to:

Reprint Permission
National Institute for Trial Advocacy
1685 38th Street, Suite 200
Boulder, CO 80301-2735
Phone: (800) 225-6482
Fax: (720) 890-7069
E-mail: permissions@nita.org
Library of Congress Cataloging-in-Publication Data

ISBN 978-1-60156-334-7
FBA 1334

14 13 12 11 10 9 8 7 6 5 4 3 2 1
Printed in the United States of America

ASPEN PUBLISHING

Official co-publisher of NITA.
aspenpublishing.com/NITA

ACKNOWLEDGMENTS

The authors would like to acknowledge the special contributions to the development of this case file made by Tahnee Baker, Alexander Lee, and Jeremy K. Heebner, law students at Pacific McGeorge School of Law, University of Pacific, who conducted research and have edited all portions of this case file.

We also wish to thank Professor Thomas Jay Leach of Pacific McGeorge School of Law, University of the Pacific for the many suggestions he has made to the development of this case file.

Thanks also to the 1947 St. Louis Browns baseball team for providing the names of many of the characters in the *Huntington v. Aster* case file.

Contents

Introduction

The plaintiff, Rose Huntington, age sixty-eight, is suing the defendant attorney Mark Aster for professional negligence, breach of fiduciary duty, conversion, and set aside of irrevocable trust. She alleges that the defendant was an attorney with the firm that previously represented her daughter April in a divorce action and claims that the defendant and April were romantically involved with each other. During that relationship, the defendant and April arranged for the defendant to meet with Rose. At the meeting, the defendant convinced Rose to convert her will to an irrevocable trust. The beneficiaries of the will were Rose's three children: April, John, and Warren, who was named as executor. The liquid value of the estate was approximately $1,500,000 in a brokerage account with Ace Investments. Under the trust, it was expected that Rose would be the lifetime beneficiary and receive all interest and dividends from the Ace brokerage account. Rose's three children were beneficiaries of the trust, with the trust res to be distributed to them in equal shares upon Rose's death. April was named the trustee to serve without bond. Rose claims that when she signed the trust, she did not understand it and the defendant did not explain the ramifications of an irrevocable trust.

Rose further alleges that April paid the defendant's fee and a retainer totaling $2,500 from April's personal checking account, and April and the defendant continued their dating relationship, which included going to a weekend resort vacation. One month after signing the trust, Rose and April had a heated argument. Rose contacted the defendant and advised him that she wanted to revoke the trust, and the defendant informed her that she couldn't do so, as the trust is irrevocable. Two weeks later, April moved out of the Huntington family home. Rose received only about two-thirds of her regular $8,000 monthly check and learned that April, with the assistance of the defendant, withdrew $750,000 from the Ace account to be placed in a more diversified account. Shortly afterwards, April and the defendant traveled to Ft. Lauderdale, Florida to consider and discuss investing in two projects in Peru. They then traveled to Peru and stayed at a resort. On the first trip to Peru the entire $750,000 was invested in the two projects. While in Peru on the second occasion, April and the defendant were scuba diving when April disappeared. An investigation by Peruvian police was unable to determine whether April died while scuba diving or whether she disappeared by her own volition or was kidnapped. Repeated efforts to locate her have failed.

The defendant claims that the trust he arranged contained many benefits and improvements over the will, and declaring the trust irrevocable protected the assets from the reach of creditors. He claims that April made the decision to invest in the Peruvian projects and he did not in any way advise her to do so. He denies that he was in any way the cause of her disappearance, and has stated that he did everything he could to find her.

The defendant was previously sued for legal malpractice and has two Nita State Bar disciplinary matters, one for failure to communicate with his client and another for co-mingling personal funds with a client trust account.

Both the plaintiff and the defendant have retained attorneys who will testify as experts on behalf of their clients.

The applicable law is set out in the sections entitled Applicable Statutory Law and Jury Instructions, set forth at the end of the file.

This is a fictional case file and is not in any way intended to represent facts in any existing factual situation.

All years in these materials are stated in the following form:

YR-0 indicates the actual year in which the case is being tried (i.e., the present year);

YR-1 indicates the next preceding year (please use the actual year);

YR-2 indicates the second preceding year (please use the actual year), etc.

Electronic files for the exhibits are available for download here:

Website: http://bit.ly/1P20Jea
Password: Huntington1

Special Instructions For Use As A Full Trial

When this case file is used for a full trial, each party is limited to calling the following witnesses:

Plaintiff: Rose Huntington

Pat Hardesty

Courtney Brown

Defendant: Mark Aster

Ashley Price

Harry Zoldak

If the case file is used for less than a full trial, each party is limited to calling the following witnesses:

Plaintiff: Rose Huntington

Pat Hardesty

(The deposition of Courtney Brown may be deemed to have been read to the jury)

Defendant: Mark Aster

Ashley Price

(The deposition of Harold Zoldak may be deemed to have been read to the jury)

Required Stipulations:

1. The plaintiff Rose Huntington and April Huntington are female. The defendant Mark Aster and Harry Zoldak are male. All other witnesses may be either male or female.

2. The Nita State Bar Disciplinary Reports Case No. YR-6-2,071 and Case No. YR-3-695 are accurate and authentic records of the disciplinary actions brought against the Defendant by the Nita State Bar Association.

3. The statement of April Huntington, taken by investigator Albert Zarilla, is authentic and an accurate account of what April Huntington stated to Mr. Zarilla, and it does not require authentication by Zarilla.

4. Exhibit 18 is an accurate photographic depiction of April Huntington.

5. General damages will not exceed $750,000. Any other damage issues are reserved for a subsequent proceeding.

Pre-trial Motions:

1. The court has ruled that Exhibit 14, the statement given by April Huntington to investigator Albert Zarilla, shall not be subject to a hearsay objection as the court has found that April Huntington's disappearance and the good faith efforts of both parties in seeking to summon her appearance as a witness establishes her unavailability under FRE 804. The court further finds that such testimony meets the three

components of FRE 807 and will be admissible under that section. This ruling does not preclude either party from interposing an objection on some ground other than hearsay. Such admissible testimony may be offered by reading the testimony into the record.

2. Exhibit 17, the Peruvian Police Missing Persons Report as translated, is an exact and authentic copy of the original document and authentication is sufficient and established under Federal Rules of Evidence Sections 901, 902, and 903.

3. All other legal issues will be ruled on by the court, either directly before trial begins or during trial.

Glen W. Moulder, Esq.
Moulder and Fannin LLP
33 Professional Drive
Nita City, Nita 85517

Attorneys for Plaintiff
ROSE HUNTINGTON

DISTRICT COURT OF THE STATE OF NITA

FOR THE COUNTY OF DARROW

ROSE HUNTINGTON, Plaintiff, v. MARK ASTER, Defendant.	Case Number: **DC-YR-2-2419CIV** **COMPLAINT FOR PROFESSIONAL NEGLIGENCE; BREACH OF FIDUCIARY DUTY; CONVERSION; AND DECLARATION THAT IRREVOCABLE TRUST BE SET ASIDE** (JURY TRIAL DEMANDED)

Plaintiff, ROSE HUNTINGTON, complains of defendant, MARK ASTER, and alleges as follows:

FIRST CAUSE OF ACTION
Professional Negligence

I.

Plaintiff, Rose Huntington, is an individual and is now, and at all times mentioned in this complaint was, a resident of Darrow County, State of Nita.

II.

Defendant, Mark Aster, is an individual and is now, and at all times mentioned in this complaint was, a resident of Darrow County, State of Nita.

III.

At all times mentioned in this complaint, defendant Mark Aster was licensed to practice law in the State of Nita.

IV.

On or about October 4, YR-2 plaintiff employed defendant to review her estate plan. Plaintiff told defendant that she wished all her estate to pass onto to plaintiff's three children in equal shares.

V.

Defendant prepared a trust, and on the advice of defendant, plaintiff executed a trust prepared by defendant.

VI.

Defendant failed to use reasonable skill and care in drafting plaintiff's trust in that defendant negligently and carelessly:

(a) Prepared an irrevocable trust and failed to properly advise plaintiff of the consequences of such a trust;

(b) Failed to advise plaintiff of the legal consequences of naming a family member and beneficiary of the trust as trustee of the trust; and

(c) Prepared a trust that waived a bond that would have indemnified the trust for certain acts of malfeasance by the trustee

VII.

As a direct and proximate result of the negligence and carelessness of defendant as set forth above, plaintiff has suffered damage in that she has been deprived of the benefits she would have received under the trust had defendant used proper skill and care in drafting the trust in accordance with plaintiff's express wishes.

VIII.

Plaintiff is informed and believes, and on the basis of that information and belief alleges, that had defendant used proper skill and care in drafting the trust in accordance with plaintiff's wishes, plaintiff's receipt of benefits and those of her beneficiaries under plaintiff's trust would not have been diminished.

SECOND CAUSE OF ACTION

Breach of Fiduciary Duty

IX.

Plaintiff incorporates by reference the allegations stated in Paragraphs 1 through 5, inclusive, as if fully set forth.

X.

At all times relevant, defendant created and acted in a fiduciary relationship of great trust as attorney for plaintiff.

XI.

Defendant breached the fiduciary duty owed to plaintiff in that defendant had a relationship with the trustee of the trust, and assisted her interests to the detriment of plaintiff.

XII.

As a result of defendant's breach of fiduciary duty, plaintiff has suffered economic detriment and damage.

THIRD CAUSE OF ACTION

Conversion

XIII.

Plaintiff incorporates by reference the allegations stated in Paragraphs 1 through 5, inclusive, as if fully set forth.

XIV.

In bringing this action pursuant to Nita State Probate Code § 466, plaintiff asserts the right to possession of certain personal property of the irrevocable trust, to wit: the sum of $1,500,000.00, that sum being the funds that were on deposit in the Ace Investment account in the name of the plaintiff on the date that the trust was entered into, and subsequently transferred into the name of The Rose Huntington Irrevocable Trust.

XV.

On or about December 5, YR-3, defendant removed $1,500,000.00 from the Ace Investment account, and transferred said funds to The Rose Huntington Irrevocable Trust.

XVI.

Subsequently, defendant released $750,000.000 of the funds to April Huntington, Trustee. Said transfer of funds constituted an actual and substantial interference with plaintiff's ownership interest in the property.

XVII.

Defendant converted said funds to his or a third party's own use.

FOURTH CAUSE OF ACTION

Declaration That Irrevocable Trust Be Set Aside

XVIII.

Plaintiff incorporates by reference the allegations stated in Paragraphs 1 through 5, inclusive, as if fully set forth.

XIX.

This lawsuit is based upon Nita Probate Code § 466, in that this irrevocable trust was executed based upon negligence, breach of fiduciary duty, undue influence, conversion, and/or conspiracy.

XX.

In the event that plaintiff prevails on any theory or any other basis upon which the trust may possibly be set aside, the court shall enter a declaration that the irrevocable trust be set aside.

WHEREFORE, plaintiff requests judgment on all causes of action against defendant, Mark Aster, for the following:

1. General damages in the amount of $750,000.00;
2. Declaration that the irrevocable trust be set aside;

3. Interest according to proof;

4. Costs of this action; and

5. Any other and further relief that the court deems just and proper.

Dated: May 17, YR-2

Glen W. Moulder, Esq.

Glen W. Moulder, Esq.
Moulder and Fannin LLP
Attorneys for Plaintiff
ROSE HUNTINGTON

Phillip McQuillen, Esq.
Frederica Sanford, Esq.
McQuillen & Sanford
323 Nita City Drive
Nita City, Nita 85518

Attorneys for Defendant
MARK ASTER

DISTRICT COURT OF THE STATE OF NITA
FOR THE COUNTY OF DARROW

ROSE HUNTINGTON, Plaintiff, v. MARK ASTER, Defendant.	Case Number: **DC-YR-2-2419CIV** **ANSWER TO COMPLAINT FOR PROFESSIONAL NEGLIGENCE; BREACH OF FIDUCIARY DUTY; CONVERSION; AND DECLARATION THAT IRREVOCABLE TRUST BE SET ASIDE** **(JURY TRIAL DEMANDED)**

COMES NOW defendant, MARK ASTER, and in answer to the Complaint for Professional Negligence, Breach of Fiduciary Duty, Conversion, and Declaration That Irrevocable Trust Be Set Aside on file herein, admits, denies, and alleges as follows:

Defendant admits the allegations set forth in paragraphs I, II, III, IV, V, IX, XIII, and XVIII of said complaint.

Defendant denies the allegations set forth in paragraphs VI, VII, VIII, X, XI, XII, XIV, XV, XVI, XVII, XIX, and XX of said complaint.

Defendant denies that plaintiff has suffered damages in the amount alleged, or in any amount.

This answering defendant hereby reserves the right to amend his answer to assert any other defenses, affirmative or otherwise, that may become available during discovery proceedings in this case.

PRAYER

WHEREFORE, defendant prays for judgment as follows:

1. That plaintiff take nothing by way of the Complaint on file herein;
2. That defendant be awarded judgment against plaintiff and awarded his costs herein incurred; and
3. That defendant be awarded such further and other relief as this court deems just and proper.

Dated: June 6, YR-2

Phillip McQuillen, Esq.

Phillip McQuillen, Esq.

Frederica Sanford, Esq.

Frederica Sanford, Esq.
Attorneys for Defendant
MARK ASTER

Glen W. Moulder, Esq.
Moulder and Fannin LLP
33 Professional Drive
Nita City, Nita 85517

Attorneys for Plaintiff
ROSE HUNTINGTON

DISTRICT COURT OF THE STATE OF NITA
FOR THE COUNTY OF DARROW

ROSE HUNTINGTON, Plaintiff, v. MARK ASTER, Defendant.	Case Number: **DC-YR-2-2419CIV** **RESTRAINING ORDER**

The matter of plaintiff's order to show cause for a restraining order pending trial came on regularly for hearing as reflected in the minutes of the court. Present was GLEN W. MOULDER, of MOULDER and FANNIN representing the plaintiff, and PHILLIP McQUILLEN, of McQUILLEN & SANFORD representing the defendant.

With the request by for a restraining order being stipulated to in open court by and through counsel for defendant, and with the matter being submitted, and good cause appearing therefore;

IT IS HEREBY ORDERED that the defendant, MARK ASTER, is restrained from transferring, encumbering, hypothecating, disposing of, or otherwise taking any action what so ever concerning any and all assets of The Rose Huntington Irrevocable Trust including investments of that trust, pending further order of court.

Dated: June 15, YR-2

Fontaine A. Goodfellow

JUDGE OF THE DISTRICT COURT

Deposition of Mark Aster

MARK ASTER, called to testify on deposition by the plaintiff and having been fully informed of all rights and obligations and duly sworn, testified as follows (objections omitted):

My name is Mark Aster. I'm not married and have no children. I currently reside in Greenville, Nita. I recently moved to Greenville after living for several years in Nita City, a few hundred miles from Greenville. I am an attorney at law, having attended Nita University School of Law and graduating with my law degree about seven years ago.

The law school was in Nita City, so I stayed there after graduation and was fortunate to find a job with Johnson & Kline, a well-established law firm. I was there for a couple of years doing mostly estate planning and general civil practice. I left that law firm under less than favorable conditions. The firm was sued for malpractice on one of my cases, which involved a situation where it was alleged that I was negligent in the preparation of an estate plan. It was a complicated case with a very influential family. The allegation was not true, but it was claimed that I caused the estate to suffer some unnecessary tax liability and that I engaged in conduct that caused further damage to the estate. I can't discuss the specifics any further due to the attorney/client privilege. The malpractice case was filed, but was settled shortly after filing. The settlement contained a confidentiality agreement.

When I left that firm, I moved to the Westin Law Firm and did some family law and general civil practice. In YR-6, the Nita State Bar filed disciplinary proceedings against me for failure to communicate with a client in a trust case. I disputed that claim, but I eventually stipulated to a Nita State Bar court order and was placed on probation for two years. At the end of that period, I was found to have completed probation successfully.

That firm completely supported me and I continued to practice until YR-3, when a personal injury client filed a claim that I had comingled trust funds. There simply was no basis for that claim. A secretary had withdrawn $5,000 from the wrong account, but since I was the client's lawyer, the Nita State Bar filed disciplinary proceedings against me. When the Bar conducted their investigation, they realized that there was no intent on my part to utilize any of the funds for personal use and they simply ordered me to attend and complete what they called the LAP, the Lawyers Assistance Program. The problem for me was because I had received two disciplinary actions in a three-year period, the firm let me go. I personally deny both claims, but I had no choice.

Shortly thereafter, I decided to get away and came to Greenville with the intent of starting a general practice of my own. I have now moved to Greenville and set up a small practice specializing in estate planning and general civil practice. I was pleased to find that I could put "specializing" on my business cards and paperwork, even though I am not a "certified specialist" with the Nita State Bar. As long as I do not state "certified specialist", I'm okay. Starting a new business in Greenville has been challenging to say the least. I was initially in need of finding new clients so that I could pay my bills. I have handled a number of cases involving estate planning, including wills and trusts, which is a pretty straight-forward practice, generally not too complicated. You know, you can charge a substantial attorney fee for a trust. In reality, most of it involves purchasing software, which you edit according to the client's specific information and it spits out the final product. Then you have the client come into your office, sign the document, and that's it. These trusts run many pages, so believe me no one reads the whole thing. You just summarize it and it's fine.

In addition to estate planning, I have handled other cases, including a few personal injury cases. One in particular concluded quite successfully. My client was test-driving a used car the dealer was offering for sale. The brakes on the car failed and my client slammed into the side of a large beer truck. My client suffered numerous injuries and there were significant damages. We sued both the driver/owner of the truck and the dealer that was selling the car. My fees were 40% of the recovery, plus expenses. My share of the settlement amounted to $237,057. Additionally, I have enough other income that I have earned over the last two years that enabled me to purchase a new home.

I came to hear about Rose Huntington through April, her daughter. I had known April before I moved to Greenville, as she had been a client of the Westin Law Firm for her divorce. I wasn't the attorney of record on her case, but I did appear with her in court on a couple of motions. We actually hit it off pretty good, but I was an attorney in the law firm, so ethical rules prohibited me from pursuing any kind of a relationship. I had heard that she had moved to Greenville, so I anticipated seeing her sometime. As it turned out, shortly after moving to Greenville, I ran into April one night when I had stopped into a local bar after work. I was happy to see her, and she appeared pleased to see me too. After that, we would meet up at the bar after work, and would have dinner together three or four nights a week. I guess I would call it a serious relationship, but we were not engaged or anything. She lived with her mother and was out of work, so I had her occasionally come and work for me at the office doing filing and such.

One evening when we were out at Jason's Tavern, April brought up the fact that Rose had a lot of money and that her attorney, Seth Middleton, had recently passed away. April suggested we have her in to review her assets and estate plan. I thought that was a good idea and I could pick up another client that way. It was April's idea. She brought up the subject. I had my calendar with me and we decided upon a convenient time for us all to meet. Our thought was to get Rose's client file from Middleton's office, which was in the process of closing.

The next day I prepared the Authorization for Release of Client File, which April took to get Rose's signature on and to use to retrieve the file. April obtained Rose's file, but apparently Rose doesn't remember signing the authorization. April brought the file to my office and I took a look at it. The file had various documents concerning the residence, the timberland, and the investment account with Ace Investments. It also contained the original will of Rose Huntington. I reviewed the will and determined that a trust would be a better approach to Rose's situation. I prefer a trust. A trust has many advantages to a will. It benefits the client, and since I am preparing it, I can make sure that it is enforceable and valid. Among the other advantages would be that it is confidential, it does not have to be witnessed, it avoids probate, and it can provide protection from creditors.

I met with Rose two times. At our first meeting, she did not request that a trust be prepared for her. She's an older lady and her daughter April was the motivating factor in her reviewing her estate. I assumed that April had discussed the matter with Rose, and that it was Rose's decision to come in for the review. I commenced preparing the trust. As I stated earlier, I prefer trusts as the best mechanism to deal with property upon one's passing away. You know, you hardly see any wills these days, as trusts are the way to go.

The will that Seth Middleton prepared was valid. It could have used a little updating. For instance, Rose's son Warren was named as the executor of the will, and in the trust, April was named as trustee. Rose never requested that April be named as the trustee. April was there with her mother. I asked her if she was willing to act as trustee and she answered in the affirmative. It seemed obvious that April was helping out her mom here and taking charge, so she was the logical person to be trustee. Besides that, April lived in Greenville with her mother.

The trust does not require that the trustee post a bond to insure that the assets are protected in the trust. The posting of a bond was waived under the terms of the trust. This is standard procedure where a close relative is nominated as trustee. Besides that, such bonds are expensive as the premiums are based on the value of the estate. The trust I prepared was an "irrevocable trust," which means that the trust cannot be revoked by the trustor, in this case Rose. An irrevocable trust protects assets. If a trust is irrevocable, when coupled with other spendthrift provisions, it means that creditors of Rose cannot reach the trust assets in order to satisfy their respective claims. It preserves the estate for the beneficiaries of the trust. I wouldn't say there is a downside to having an irrevocable trust. As the name indicates, the trust cannot be revoked so the trust and its terms remain in effect until such time as the trustor passes away. Yes, it is true that even if later on Rose wanted to revoke the trust, she could not do so and thus her property in the trust would remain in the trust. And that is precisely why creditors of Rose cannot reach the assets of the trust, as the assets that were transferred into the trust remain trust assets, and thus not Rose's personal assets subject to her creditors. I don't believe that she had any such creditors. Although, that's not to say that she might not incur some in the future.

Rose did come back for a second appointment, and, of course, April was present at the second appointment. April brought her. I explained the trust to Rose. Rose appeared to understand the terms of the trust and what it was intended to do. April was also in the room and was trying to explain it so her, so that Rose would feel more confident. Rose kept asking about whether all three children would receive equal amounts of her money. And I kept on repeating that Warren, John, and April would all receive equal shares. I must say she asked me that so many times that I got a bit frustrated. In the room when the trust was signed were Rose, April and Courtney Brown. I was there too. Courtney Brown is a notary public, who was there to notarize the document. Courtney arrived right at the same time when Rose and April came to my office. Courtney came in at the beginning of the interview and sat patiently waiting until it was time to perform notary duties by witnessing Rose's signature. I charged Rose $2,500 for the trust. I recognize Exhibit 1 as the trust that I have referred to in this testimony. Assuming Rose's will was to be revised, I would have billed $250 for such a revision. April was concerned that her mother would become irritated with her because of the cost, so she wrote me a check for the $2,500. That was her choice, and I did not object.

Approximately one month after the trust was signed, Rose contacted me. I hadn't heard from Rose at all since the signing of the trust. One day, out of the blue, she called me and seemed quite distraught. Apparently, she had a falling out of sorts with April the night before, and she was so worried that she wanted to revoke the trust and go back to a will like the one that Seth Middleton had prepared. I told her that the trust was irrevocable and that she could not simply revoke the trust at this point in time. I tried to talk with her further, but Rose seemed very frustrated and hung up the phone. I tried to call her back, but she did not answer.

After this call, I talked with April about the trust and her duties as a trustee. April was working in my office doing filing kinds of tasks, and we had been going out to drinks and dinner on a regular basis. During the next two weeks, I came to understand that April, as trustee, was going to move some of the funds out of the Ace Investment account into another investment. In fact, I assisted April, as trustee, in withdrawing some of the funds from the Ace Investment account as she indicated that she wanted to invest some of those funds in a business venture. She had asked me if I was aware of any investments that would produce more income than the Ace Investment. I told her that I knew of some, including investments in areas of high growth in other countries. This was not unusual. Many investors were looking to overseas investments for greater appreciation than could be found in the U.S. I advised her that the funds were trust assets and must remain as such. I also advised her that she must use prudent business judgment in investing the assets. I assisted her in obtaining the funds, making sure that the funds were withdrawn and made payable to, "April Huntington, trustee of The Rose Huntington Irrevocable Trust." I assumed that she would follow my advice. The completion of the withdrawal of trust funds from the Ace Investment account occurred approximately two weeks after the telephone call from Rose. Exhibits 2 and 3 are the checks withdrawing $500,000 and then $250,000 from The Ace Investment Account and placing that money in my Attorney Client Trust Account.

I took steps to notify Rose of the withdrawal from the Ace Investment account. I called her and she seemed surprised that April could do such a thing. Rose asked how April could do this withdrawal, and I told her that a trustee has the power to move and re-invest assets of a trust. By the time that the withdrawal occurred, I had moved the Ace Investment account to my Attorney Client Trust account, and then into the name of the trust. That would be appropriate standard procedure. All trust assets must be in the name of the trust. Rose seemed surprised when she heard this as well. I don't know that she knew that such action would be taken. I didn't feel it was necessary to take steps to advise Rose in advance of the withdrawal of part of the investment from the Ace Investment account, since the assets were in an irrevocable trust. As far as I knew, April was acting totally within her granted powers as trustee. It is true that on April's request, funds had been withdrawn from the Ace Investment Account for The Rose Huntington Irrevocable Trust, then transferred to my Attorney Client Trust Account, and then transferred to April Huntington, Trustee for The Rose Huntington Irrevocable Trust Account at Nita National Bank.

Shortly after the two checks totaling $750,000 were transferred to April as trustee, I became concerned about my position as trust protector of The Rose Huntington Irrevocable Trust. At the outset, I had thought that I could act as a trust protector in this case without any complications. However, as time progressed, my relationship with April became more serious. Ethically, it appeared to me that I should no longer act as trust protector with April acting as trustee. I recalled that the trust gave the trust protector the authority to resign at any time at his or her sole discretion. I decided that this was the best thing to do under the circumstances and I resigned as trust protector effectively immediately. I notified Rose and April by mail of my resignation.

About a week later, April told me she was very excited about Peruvian investments, and said that she had spoken with an investment firm that recommended a new coastal resort project called La Costa Magnifica and also a development company called the Peruvian Land and Mining Company. She said that she had contacted a man named Alfonso Escobar, who was brokering investments in this area, and said that he would be happy to meet with her when he was in Ft. Lauderdale the following week. She asked me to accompany her and asked if I thought that expenses for the trip would be covered under the trust. I told her that they would be proper so long as that was the reason for the trip. I told her that I would go. We flew to Ft. Lauderdale, stayed at a nice but not overly expensive hotel, and had two rather protracted conversations with Mr. Escobar. My chief concern was that any funds invested in overseas projects be insured, either by a U.S. company or by the national government involved. Mr. Escobar assured us that these were joint projects approved by the Peruvian government and any written agreement would include such guarantees. Mr. Escobar showed us documents that projected a minimum of 17% income on an annual basis. On the third day, we flew back to Nita and returned to Greenville.

It was not my position to decide the issue, as April was the trustee. After thinking about it for a day, April called me and said she had called Mr. Escobar and made arrangements for the two of us to fly to Peru and stay at La Costa Magnifica. She arranged an appointment with three representatives: one from the government, one from the land and mining company, and one from the resort. The next week we flew to Peru and stayed at La Costa Magnifica. We were both impressed with the facility and the location. In fact, we tried scuba diving off the coast. It was truly a beautiful place and there appeared to be a number of tourists at the resort, including Americans. Again, we were assured that the government was completely behind both projects. As for the mining and land venture, it appeared to be very expansive, with new development of copper, coal mining, and land development in previously undeveloped areas. The income projections appeared to be very promising and squared with what Mr. Escobar had told us.

April informed me that she wanted to invest the entire $750,000, with $250,000 to go to the resort and $500,000 to go to the government mining and land project. I tried to caution her that a more conservative approach would be the best way to go in case something bad happened in the Peruvian economy. I explained the concept of diversification. April was headstrong and said she would be very sorry if she didn't take full advantage of the opportunity. April told me that she, as trustee for the trust, then contacted the Nita National Bank and made arrangements to have the agreed upon funds electronically transferred immediately to the local bank nearby in Mancora, Peru. Exhibits 6 and 7 appear to be the electronic transfers that she arranged. She also told me that a written agreement had already been drawn up for each investment. Apparently, April then paid each of the representatives the agreed upon amount. As I recall it, the payments were paid by wire transfer. That evening in Mancora, we all dined at a fine restaurant at their expense. I have to admit that La Costa Magnifica was a very impressive resort. In fact, in the late afternoon I wandered around the resort area and spoke with the concierge of the resort. He suggested I look at the art works of Julio Garza, a renowned Peruvian artist. He told me that Garza had a studio nearby. When I looked at his artwork, I found a watercolor painting displaying the resort, which I bought. Exhibit 9 is that painting. I did not take any photos of the place, but we returned with one photo that the resort's scuba instructor took of April under water. Exhibit 8 is that photo. Exhibit 18 is an accurate photo of April. The next day, we returned to the States.

April and I agreed that we should return again in a month to check the progress of both investments. We did this. Throughout this time, Rose remained exceedingly angry about April's decision and even suggested that she might retain a lawyer and sue me. Obviously this worried me, so I retained an investigator, Albert Zarilla, to obtain a complete statement from April confirming what April had done to ensure that this was a sound investment. Exhibit 14 is the statement I am referring to.

The next month, April and I returned to La Costa Magnifica and because we had so enjoyed scuba diving the last time, the first thing we did after breakfast was go for a dive using dive equipment from the resort. We dived off the coast just north of the resort. I was only moderately experienced in scuba diving, but April told me that she had taken a class in scuba diving when she attended Glendale Valley Community College. From the way she dived the first time in Peru, she looked like a pro.

We went off together. We were told that two people always should stay together. However, I was particularly interested in an area that we discovered on our first visit. There was an incredible array of brightly colored fish that had surrounded us. April, on the other hand, said that she was interested in exploring an area of caves and rocks. So we agreed to separate for the beginning of the dive and agreed that I would then go over to the caves area about fifteen or twenty minutes later and meet her. Actually, I probably spent close to one-half hour swimming through the lush area of plants and fish and then headed back to the caves area. When I got there I couldn't find April. I began to get worried, and decided perhaps I had the wrong area, so I quickly canvassed the areas on both sides of the caves. There was no sign of April anywhere. I returned to the caves area and entered two or three caves. Again, no sign of April. That's when I began to panic. I then immediately swam back to the shore and yelled for the lifeguards.

There were lifeguards in the area, as there were rocks at the point and the beach nearby. I asked the two lifeguards if they had seen April return. They said they had not, but they had just returned to that area after spending about a half hour further down the coast admonishing swimmers that the surf in that area was dangerous. The two lifeguards then got diving gear, and immediately swam out towards the area where April and I had been diving. The lifeguards searched the entire area, and not only did they not see April, there was no evidence of any kind that she had been there. No equipment or clothing of any kind was seen anywhere. The two lifeguards suggested we immediately return to La Costa Magnifica to see if she returned to the resort. We got back and I immediately checked our room. Not only was April not there, her belongings were gone. I searched everywhere, and I found nothing of hers. She had copies of the signed documents. They were gone. She used two suitcases on the trip and had a purse. They were all gone.

I went to the front desk and talked with the clerk. He said that April had not checked out, and he had not seen her either enter the hotel or leave it. He told me he did not make any attempt to visually check people in and out, and also said there was a rear entrance and exit that was not visible from the front desk.

I didn't know what to do. My first thought was perhaps she was kidnapped or even murdered. April had never given me even a hint that she would voluntarily leave. The only thing I knew to do was to call the American Embassy, and they suggested that I report her missing to the police, and they told me that there were recent kidnappings of Americans in two different areas of central Peru, and it could be possible that this could be happening in other tourist areas. I then thought that kidnappers could have taken her back to the hotel, removed her belongings, and then made their escape. I was totally panicked. The hotel manager said they would drive me to the police station. As we were leaving La Costa Magnifica I was amazed to hear the hotel security officer murmur something about maybe I was the one who caused her disappearance. In fact, he said something about how I might be a van der Sloot.

We drove to the nearest police station which was in Mancora. I don't speak Spanish, so our driver spoke with the front desk and explained the circumstances, and I then spoke with an officer who understood English. I told him what happened, and he said that he would pass this on to the chief. Shortly after that Police Chief Diego spoke with me and said that they would consider this a missing person case, but before they came to a decision they would have to rule out that there was a criminal act. I then sat down with Detective Villegas who spoke English. I explained in detail the background and why we came to La Costa Magnifica. We discussed the investments and I gave him the names of all the people involved in the investment agreements. He then drove me back to the hotel. I told him what the embassy staff told me, and I asked that he conduct an investigation to find out who kidnapped her and where they were holding her. The detective spoke to people at the front desk and then I went with him to the hotel room. He asked me why I did not have copies of the investment documents, and I explained that April was the trustee, and she was the only one who had the authority to sign. I told him the documents and April's belongings were in the room when we left to go scuba diving, and they were missing when I came back. Detective Villegas told me that I would not be permitted to leave Peru until they completed their investigation, and asked me to attempt to get some verification that the negotiations I had described were in fact conducted. It felt like the police were completely ignoring the thought of a kidnapping and were even believing that I was involved in the disappearance.

I tried to get more information about the investments, but when I spoke to the manager at La Costa Magnifica, he said that he did not know Daniela Medina, who was the representative of the resort. I then contacted the Peruvian Land and Mining Company, and I was told that they had no one by the name of Gustavo Vega working for their firm. I then reported this to the police department when they said I could return to the States. I have since requested in writing from both the resort and the Peruvian Land and Mining Company certified documents verifying that there are no records of such agreements. It is now clear that this was a scam job from the beginning, and the people that were involved in the scan then kidnapped April. I have been unable to locate anyone by the name of Alfonso Escobar who stayed in the Beach Suites Hotel at the time we stayed there in Ft. Lauderdale. I have reviewed Exhibit 17, the Peruvian police report, and I don't disagree with most of the content, but it appears that the police department first secured the information about the documents, and that is not true. I got that information first and passed it on to the police, and they must then have called and corroborated that. I also resent their inclusion of the speculation of the hotel security officer in their official report.

April was probably the most important person in my life at that time. We had a fine relationship. I loved her company. Of course I dated other women as well. I am totally unaware of any reason why April left, and I have no idea where she went, but I do know that there wasn't a sign of any foul play and the police could find no trace of where she went. I have learned that her former husband suggested that April was devious enough to have masterminded such a scheme and may well have had a secret lover. If that is the case, I never saw anything to suggest it. I also have continued to try and locate April. I have asked everyone I know to let me know if they have any idea of her whereabouts. I have conducted Internet searches on a regular basis trying to locate her. I can only believe that for some mysterious reason, she died scuba diving and no one was able to find her, or she has in fact fled to some location, perhaps with the help of others, and all this was done to steal Rose's money. The reason I cannot rule out that possibility is that there is no other explanation for her cleaning out her belongings in the hotel room. But I certainly don't want to believe that. Of course, it is still possible that she was kidnapped and is still being held. I have read of such kidnappings in South America and specifically in Peru. I certainly have no faith that the Peruvian Police Department or the government of Peru would have conducted a thorough investigation of kidnapping. I would, in a way, prefer to believe that April conned me and made off with the money.

With all due respect, I cannot be responsible for what April may or may not have done with the trust assets. It's not disputed that the $750,000 is now unaccounted for, as the check from Ace Investments was deposited in my Attorney Client Trust account, and then transferred to the April Huntington, Trustee of The Rose Huntington Irrevocable Trust account at Nita National Bank, and then withdrawn by April and electronically transferred to Mancora. How can I possibly be responsible for her unaccountability with the trust funds? No, I absolutely do not have any of the funds and have never been in possession of those funds. That question suggests that I was in some way trying to acquire those funds. I resent the question and if you have any more questions along that line, then I'm through.

I, MARK ASTER, do certify that I have read the foregoing pages of my testimony as transcribed and that it is a true and correct transcript of the testimony given by me in this deposition on July 7, YR-2, in the offices of plaintiff's counsel.

Mark Aster

Certified by:

Maria de los Ramos
Certified Shorthand Reporter

Deposition of Ashley Price

ASHLEY PRICE, called to testify on deposition by the plaintiff and having been fully informed of all rights and obligations and duly sworn, testified as follows (objections omitted):

My name is Ashley Price. I am an attorney at law licensed to practice in the State of Nita. I have been admitted to practice for eleven years. I attended The University of Nita Law School on a three year scholarship and graduated with honors. I took the bar exam, which was administered by the State Bar of Nita, and passed the exam on my first try. In law school, I took courses in Decedent's Estates and Trusts and Professional Responsibility. Following my admission to the bar, I attended the Graziadio School of Business MBA Program at Pepperdine University, and I received my MBA degree in YR-8. I was able to complete a good deal of that program through their distance learning procedures, and I had to attend courses in Malibu only infrequently.

I began the practice of law as an associate counsel with the law offices of Berardino and Kinder in Nita City, Nita. During my three years with that firm I handled all types of cases including bankruptcy, family law, elder law, estate planning, trust, and probate law. My experience there included some litigation work, mostly in elder law and estate planning. In YR-9 I opened my own practice, and shortly thereafter I was certified by the Nita State Bar as a specialist in Estate Planning, Probate and Trusts, and Elder Law. Additionally, I have handled several legal malpractice cases.

In my eleven years of practice, I have served on two of the State Bar of Nita committees. In YR-4, I served on the Professional Responsibility Committee. In that capacity, other committee members and I reviewed the handling of bar disciplinary cases involving practitioners in a number of fields including estate planning, probate, and trust law. We made recommendations for improving both reporting and investigation of such cases, and we made recommendations concerning dispositions of such cases. In YR-2, I was appointed to the Executive Department Liaison Committee, a committee that makes recommendations to the Office of the Governor of The State of Nita concerning both administrative regulations and proposed new legislation. At least some of the matters that we dealt with included estate planning and probate law.

I have given presentations in my areas of specialization to members of the bar, to citizens groups, and to business professionals. Additionally, I have been published on two occasions in the area of trusts and estate planning.

I have testified in court as an expert witness on six occasions. Approximately four years ago I testified as an expert for the defense in a trust and probate case, *Estate of Snyder v. Fitzpatrick*. Since that time I have been qualified as an expert in trust and probate matters in two other cases, as an expert in an elder law case, and in two cases of legal malpractice involving estate planning issues. As a result of my work in those two cases, I was honored to receive a prestigious award as an outstanding expert in that area. Those were all cases heard in the State of Nita District Court here in Nita City. Yes, in each instance I appeared for the defense, though I certainly have no bias against serving as an expert for plaintiffs. In my practice, I have prepared hundreds of wills and trusts. I do not personally know anyone related to the present case. Exhibit 15 is an accurate and current version of my C.V. To prepare my opinion in this matter I reviewed Exhibits 1 through 17 along with Mark Aster's deposition.

In reviewing The Rose Huntington Irrevocable Trust, Exhibit 1, I have the following observations. In basic terms, it is a "garden variety" trust. There is nothing odd or unusual about it. From my own experience I can tell that it was generated from the same software that I use in my practice. In my experience, virtually all attorneys use this type of software to prepare trusts. This particular software is very good. You can use it with very little editing, except for adding some specificity as to the property going into the trust. If you are going to prepare a "basic trust," you can use it pretty much as it comes installed on your computer.

I do not believe that Rose's trust presented any complicated issues. As to the naming of a trustee, often the person creating the trust, the trustor, names herself as trustee during her lifetime. On the other hand, it is perfectly normal to name a family member as the trustee. As I understand it in this case, the trustor's daughter, April, was named by Rose, or at least accepted by her, as trustee. That is fine and often done in cases where the person creating the trust is getting along in years and frankly, it is just better to have another act as trustee. April, apparently living with her mother, would seem to be a logical choice.

The issue of the posting of a bond often comes up in cases where a trustee other than the trustor herself is to be named. From my experience, bond is almost always waived in cases such as this for several reasons. A bond is to protect the trust estate from loss due to misappropriation and such. When you have a close family member acting as trustee, bond is not needed, as the likelihood of malfeasance is small. This is particularly so where the trustee is also a residual beneficiary of the trust at the time of the preparation of the trust. I would have had no qualms about waiving the bond. Not requiring a bond saves the trust a substantial amount of money each year, and as such should be factored into this analysis also.

In drafting a trust, an attorney must always consider whether the trust should be revocable or irrevocable. I have drafted both types of trusts in my practice. In fact, I have given a presentation to the State of Nita Retired Employees Association fully discussing the benefits of each type depending upon the circumstances. On one hand, it is often good to have the ability to revoke or change the trust after it is put into place. On the other hand, an irrevocable trust acts to preserve assets in the trust, particularly if there is a worry that creditors of the trustor may try to invade the trust should the trustor become indebted. One never knows what may come up, and particularly with older folks, it's often best to make the trust irrevocable. Although this does have the effect of limiting what the trustor may take out of the trust, for that same reason it serves to preserve the trust assets from creditors. The information about Rose Huntington's financial affairs and state of health that

Mr. Aster had received, as he testified in his deposition, constituted in my view a reasonable argument for the advisability of an irrevocable trust. For all these reasons it is my opinion that Mr. Aster's recommendation of an irrevocable trust was fully compliant with his duty to exercise the level of skill and care expected of attorneys practicing in Nita.

I understand that in this case, the attorney who drafted the trust has been placed in the trust as a "trust protector." This is someone nominated by the trustor to oversee and protect the trust. This person is in a position to work closely with the trustee. The trust protector must always act with the trust's interest foremost in mind, while at the same time assisting the trustee in her duties. This can be a difficult position. I have avoided being nominated as a trust protector in my cases. This may be proper and appropriate in some cases. As a lawyer, I do not want to take on any liability as a trust protector. I do think that a trust protector should not be liable for the independent actions of the trustee.

I understand that in this case Mr. Aster resigned as trust protector shortly after the checks were withdrawn from his client trust account and made payable to April as trustee. The trust is clear that the trust protector has the sole discretion to resign at any time. Once he resigned his duties as trust protector are concluded.

I reviewed Rose's earlier will which was prepared by Seth Middleton and revoked by the subsequent trust. The will met all of the requirements of the Nita probate statutes and was valid in all respects. However, compared to the will, the trust that Mr. Aster recommended to Mrs. Huntington, which it appears she accepted after hearing a full explanation of its provisions, acts to protect the estate from creditors and avoids substantial probate costs. If this is what the client wanted, in my opinion to a reasonable degree of legal certainty it was an appropriate choice. The plaintiff's expert states the view that Mr. Aster did not sufficiently advise Mrs. Huntington about the pros and cons of the trust and in particular about its irrevocability aspects. I disagree. From his description of their two meetings, it is my opinion that he made all efforts required of a reasonably competent lawyer to explain the course of action to the client. Apparently there arose some bad feelings between Rose and April shortly after the execution of the trust, which could explain what appears to be a case of "buyer's remorse" on Mrs. Huntington's part.

I am aware that this case involves accusations that Mark Aster acted improperly by having a romantic relationship with the trustee April Huntington. While I would generally counsel against entering into such a relationship because of what the law terms the "appearance of impropriety," there is no ethical rule against it. The rules forbid only sexual relationships with "a client," which April was not. I also understand from his testimony that Mr. Aster says no such relationship existed. I do not serve as the decision-maker on such disputed factual issues. I merely offer my professional opinion that even if the allegation is true, it does not arise to the level of professional misconduct.

I am also aware that there are accusations that Mark Aster improperly and illegally conspired with April Huntington to act contrary to Rose Huntington's best interests by reallocation certain investments of the trust funds, which led to their substantial diminution, and/or by using funds for their joint travel to Florida and Peru. As to the investments, neither the attorney who drafts a proper trust, as Mr. Aster did here, nor the trustee is considered a warrantor of the performance of the trust investments. The travel expenses appear to have been for a proper purpose, for the investigation of the proposed reinvestments.

I have reviewed the content of Exhibits 10 and 11, and I see no evidence that proves any of these accusations. I am also aware of the two previous Nita State Bar disciplinary matters covered in Exhibits 12 and 13. My opinion that Mr. Aster reacted properly and professionally in this matter is unchanged by any of the evidence I have reviewed.

I was retained by counsel for Mr. Aster, and so far I have devoted six hours to review of case materials and initial preparation time, and approximately four hours' time to prepare for and attend this deposition. My hourly rate is $275.00, and that will be my rate for the time spent at this deposition and if I prepare for and attend a trial.

I, ASHLEY PRICE, do hereby certify that I have read the foregoing pages of my testimony as transcribed and that it is a true and correct transcript of the testimony given by me in this deposition on July 14, YR-2, in the offices of plaintiff's counsel.

Ashley Price

Ashley Price

Certified by:

Maria de los Ramos

Maria de los Ramos
Certified Shorthand Reporter

Deposition of Harry Zoldak

HARRY ZOLDAK, called to testify on deposition by the plaintiff and having been fully informed of all rights and obligations and duly sworn, testified as follows (objections omitted):

My name is Harry Zoldak. I am a commercial real estate broker and I live in Nita City. I have a somewhat varied background. Before handling commercial real estate, I co-owned a small bar and restaurant in Nita City called The Office. My clientele consisted largely of business clients in the downtown area. Anytime they dropped into my place for a drink they were always able to tell their spouse that they were "at the office." My biggest difficulties during that time of my life consisted of having too many drinks and having too many problems in my marriage. The best thing I ever did was get sober, find religion, and divorce April Huntington.

April and I first dated about nine years ago. At the time I was working both as a car salesman and I occasionally served as an auctioneer for estate sales. April was a very attractive young woman, and I felt lucky that she found me attractive. In a short period of time, we decided to marry. We went to New Orleans for a honeymoon and then travelled throughout the Gulf Coast. When we returned, April got a job at car dealership that was a competitor of the dealership I worked for. When we returned, April got a job at a competitor car dealership. She encouraged me to consider going into my own business. She mentioned that her boss, Jeff Heath, had a brother, Dean Heath, who was interested in buying and refurbishing a downtown bar and grill. She suggested I look into that. I had saved a good deal of my earnings over the last several years and it sounded like a good investment. Dean and I got along great, and we bought the place and called it The Office. We thought that was pretty funny. So did a lot of people. For the first year, things went well. We were making a financial success of the place, but things started going sour in my marriage.

I began to get the impression that April liked to flirt with other men. This was especially so when she was around Jeff. Before long, I started suspecting that April was playing around with Jeff. I confronted April, and she got very angry, accusing me of not trusting her. That's when I started drinking too much. In the past, I never had a problem with alcohol. Occasionally I might have a drink or two too many, but I didn't handle my problems with April well. For a while, I believed April when she said she had no romantic interest in Jeff. But as time went on, people began to hint or suggest that April and Jeff seemed to be together a lot. It finally came to a head when a friend asked if April was buying a new Corvette and I said I didn't think so. The friend told me that he had seen April and Jeff together in what looked like a new Corvette, and they were parked next to Darrow Park. I got in my car and drove there. It was almost dusk. I saw them sitting at a picnic table. They were sitting next to each other on one side of the table, and it looked like April had her hand on his arm. I decided to go home, and I waited for April to come home. She did, around 9:30 at night. I asked her where she had been, and she told me she had been with two of her card playing lady friends. She said they had been playing cards and she realized it was late, so she rushed home.

Well, this was pretty devastating. I debated in my mind whether to divorce her. I ended up saying nothing. I went to my room and drank a half of a bottle of sour mash whiskey. I overslept the next morning. From that point on, I hid out in a bottle. Finally, my friends told me that I was going to kill myself with alcohol. One of my friends took me to AA. I decided to move out of the house that April and I had rented. After four weeks of sobriety, a counselor at AA suggested that I start over in real estate. He offered a suggestion that I meet with a member of AA who managed a commercial real estate office for Coldwell Banker. I interviewed, was hired, and I moved on in my life. April filed for divorce. We didn't have much in assets. Since the money invested in The Office was my separate property, I got that. I found out later that April continued her affair with Jeff until Jeff's wife found out about the two, and then he fired her.

When I was contacted by the investigator and asked to give my deposition, I agreed to do so. Now that I know that April has fled somewhere probably with three quarters of a million dollars, I don't mind sharing with others information that may explain why she did this. I feel that it is important for people to know that I believe April was two people. She appeared honest, sincere, almost vulnerable. But the other April was conniving, duplicitous, and selfish. She used to talk to me about how much money her father made, and she felt it was unfair that now that she was an adult, she didn't get a fair share of his estate. She said her mother never did anything, and didn't need that much money to live. In the beginning of our marriage, she talked about the possibility of hiring a lawyer to get her fair share of the estate.

I want everyone to understand that I don't even know Mark Aster. My impression, from what I understand about her relationship with Mr. Aster, is that April was trying to get her hands on that money from the get go. I know that people think it is possible that Mr. Aster may have been involved in her plan to steal the money. My belief is that it was April who engineered the whole plan to get the money, get her hands on it, and then use it to do what she wanted. In fact, I recall April saying in the early days of our marriage that she would love to have enough money so we could both go off to some foreign land and enjoy the good things in life like the ocean and beaches. The good April wouldn't have done that. But the bad April was fully capable of doing that. The first time I had ever heard of the expression "bi-polar" was when people described April that way. Exhibit 18 is a photo of April Huntington.

It is true that I have two criminal convictions. Both occurred in that window of time when I was married to April and both were alcohol related. I have been sober for five years now. I have been able to turn my life around, and I thank my lucky stars that I was able to get out of April's grasp. That was a nightmare period in my life. I know that I am under oath, and I would say what I said today if I were standing before the Lord.

I, HARRY ZOLKAK, do hereby certify that I have read the foregoing pages of my testimony as transcribed and that it is a true and correct transcript of the testimony given by me in this deposition on July 14, YR-2, in the offices of plaintiff's counsel.

Harry Zoldak

Certified by:

Maria de los Ramos
Certified Shorthand Reporter

Deposition of Rose Huntington

ROSE HUNTINGTON, called to testify on deposition by the defendant and having been fully informed of all rights and obligations and duly sworn, testified as follows (objections omitted):

My name is Rose Huntington. I am sixty-eight years old and have lived all of my life in Greenville, Nita. I had three children: Warren, who is forty-two and married with one child; John, who is forty and married with two children; and April, who was thirty-six and recently divorced with no children. April may have died earlier this year. Warren and John both attended fine universities and married wonderful young ladies. Both Warren and John have good jobs in Nita City, the capital city of Nita, about 200 miles from Greenville. They don't visit much as they are busy with their families and their professions.

My father, J. R. Huntington, founded the town of Greenville about eighty years ago. He founded a mining company known as the Crescent Mining Company, and along with the timber and other endeavors, was quite successful. I was the only child and led a pampered life. Both my mother and father are now deceased. Since I was their only child, I inherited all of their assets. My estate now is comprised of our old family home here in Greenville, substantial timberlands surrounding Greenville, and various investments held in an investment account at Ace Investments. For years now, I have lived off of the income produced from the investment account with Ace Investments. This income was enough for me to support my lifestyle since the old family home is paid for, and the timberlands are also free and clear of any loan. Outside of my usual living expenses, all I have to pay for are the property taxes associated with the old family home and the timber land.

I have been fairly healthy over the years. I spend most of my days at various social clubs that I belong to and having luncheons with my lady friends. My doctor, Jared Allen, tells me that physically I'm pretty good; however, he adds that sometimes my memory seems to be slipping. I do pay all of my bills, and I keep track of the investments in the Ace Investment account. I set up that brokerage account some years ago so that I wouldn't have to worry about the investments on a day-to-day basis. Ace Investments sent me a check each month from the dividends and interest income. The account usually provided about $8,000 per month, which was plenty for me to live on. I was lucky to be able to live on just the income from the Ace Investment account, that way I preserved the investment. I thought someday I might need that money to help pay for my care in a rest home if it ever comes to that. I want to live in the old family residence for as long as possible, but you never know what's in the cards. I do get a little forgetful from time to time.

About one year ago, my daughter April came to live with me for a while. She had been living and working in Nita City. That was not the first time she had financial problems and had to stay with me. I say "a while" because when she came, I didn't know how long she was going to stay. She'd been through a bad divorce from Harry and she had been having a tough time finding a good job. She thought she had a good job working for the car dealer, but her boss proved to be a skunk who used her and then tossed her out when his wife found out that the two had an affair. April was a wonderful daughter, but she really didn't choose well when it came to men. In hindsight, I wasn't too thrilled to have her move in with me, but she insisted. What was I to do, as she is my daughter and had nowhere else to go?

April wasn't around too much, which was good from my perspective. She would be out late two or three evenings a week, and then more recently on weekends occasionally she would be out all night. I know that because I'm a light sleeper. She steadily stayed out longer. I later came to learn why this was. When I would ask her where she was, she would say that she got in late, but I know that's not true. I heard from one of my lady friends that April had met a new man in town. I now know that it was Mark Aster. Apparently, he had moved to town about the same time April moved in with me.

Mark Aster is a lawyer. I have not known any lawyers other than Seth Middleton, our old family attorney. He's deceased now; passed away about eight months ago. Nice man, the whole town turned out for his funeral. I've never had much need for a lawyer. About eight years or so ago, I did have Seth draw up a will for me. It was similar to the will that my husband had before his death. I thought that would be a good thing to do, as I'm getting older now. I wanted to be sure that all three of my children would share equally in my assets should something happen to me. In the meantime, I was capable of paying my bills and taking care of myself.

I thought my current will was just fine, but April apparently thought I needed to see a lawyer about my estate and will, so she arranged an appointment with Mark Aster, her friend and the new attorney in town. I didn't know anything about it until she told me that I had an appointment to see him. I was surprised and didn't know what it was about. I had no idea why we were going to see him. April said he wanted to look over my will and talk about my estate or something of that nature. I knew that my old dear friend and attorney Seth Middleton had recently passed away, so I thought that this was something I had to do.

April took me to his office about two months after she moved back in with me. We sat down in the waiting room. The first thing Mr. Aster did was walk right up to April and gave her a big hug and whispered something to her. I don't know what he said. He welcomed me and invited us into his office. It was just the three of us in his office: April, Mark Aster, and me. He had a thick file on his desk that he kept looking through, which I later came to discover was my file from Seth Middleton's office. I was surprised to see the file, but I guess that's what happens when an attorney passes away. I asked him why I was meeting with him. He said that it was time to review my estate and will to make sure that everything was legal and enforceable. I told him that I thought that Seth Middleton was a gentleman and a fine attorney, and that I was sure that everything was fine. He said that he would see about that and said he was considering recommending to me that I have a trust instead of a will. He said he would tell me more about that at the next appointment. He didn't advise me on anything, and I felt the whole meeting was a waste of time.

The next appointment was about two weeks later. I didn't have anything to do with it. April just put me in the car one day and took me over to Mr. Aster's office. When we got there and went into his office, Courtney Brown was also there, and sat in on the whole appointment. I later came to find out that Brown was there to notarize the trust. I told Aster that I liked my current will and just wanted to leave things alone and be done with it. He said that he'd looked into it and that due to some changes in the law he thought a trust would be much better for me. He rambled on about some legal stuff, about how it would be confidential, it would avoid court, and it would protect me from creditors. I liked the confidential idea, this being such a small town, but I didn't care a hoot about the rest.

Mr. Aster brought out this document. It was long and looked complicated, too many pages to read. Well, I can't read that kind of thing, so I told him so. He said no problem, and that he would summarize it for me, and I guess he did. I told him about my concerns, but he just kept talking until I was exhausted and just wanted to get out of there. Before I signed the document, I wanted to make sure that I could remain in my residence; that I would continue to get the dividends and interest from my Ace Investments account; that I would be able to keep all of my assets; and that all three of my children, Warren, John, and April, would always share equally in my estate when I pass away. Mr. Aster told me that nothing would change except that the trust would make everything confidential and I would avoid probate court. I then signed the document, although I didn't want to, but since nothing was changing I thought it would be okay. I think now, and I thought then, that my old will that Seth prepared was just fine. Yes, Exhibit 1 looks like the document I signed. And, yes, I agree it is not a lot of pages, but at the time Mr. Aster was going on and on, it seemed like that many pages.

After leaving the office, April and I did not discuss anything about what had just occurred. I'm a private sort of person and I like to keep things private. And besides that, I was irritated that April had taken me there. I don't like lawyer kind of things, and I wasn't sure about this trust thing everyone keeps talking about. About one month later, I did bring up the trust issue that had been bothering me. I liked my old will, and I asked April why she and the attorney had pushed me so hard to sign the trust. This was in the late afternoon and I know she had been drinking, so she was a little belligerent. She got that way when she drank alcohol. So she said some unkind things to me and told me that I was much better off with the trust, as she could help me with my financial affairs, and that would be better for me.

It came as a surprise to me that she was now involved directly in my financial affairs. I've always prided myself as being a widow and able to take care of myself and my own finances. If anyone were going to assist me in my financial affairs, it would be my oldest son Warren. He was the executor of my will. In that conversation with April, she called me an "incompetent old fool," and said she was going to handle things from now on. She said some other unkind things and then she left, I suspect to go and see Mr. Aster who she regularly went out with in the evenings. By now it was getting on into the evening and I ate a little something by myself and went to bed.

This whole situation continued to bother me. The next day, I called attorney Mr. Aster and told him that I wanted to revoke the trust and have my old will back. He seemed irritated, and then he went on to tell me that I could not revoke the trust as it was in his words "an irrevocable trust," and that I would just have to live with it. He also added that my previous will had been revoked. I got so angry that I hung up the telephone and put it on silent mode, as I didn't want to talk to anybody. I considered calling my oldest son, Warren, but I couldn't bring myself to bother him as he lives out of town and has a family and such. So, I just let things go for a while. Two weeks later, when I was out at a luncheon with my lady friends, I came home to find that April had moved out. She had apparently packed up all of her belongings and was gone. No note, nothing. I never heard from her again. I suspect that she moved out and went to stay with Mark Aster.

In the next week or so, I got my usual check from my Ace Investment account. When I opened up the envelope, I couldn't believe what I saw. The check was for about two-thirds of what it usually was. The check is based on the interest and dividends from the Ace Investment account and it can vary slightly. However this check, instead of being my usual check in the amount of about $8,000 was about $5,500. I was beside myself and I called Ace Investments. They weren't even going to talk to me at first, as I am apparently not the trustee of my trust. But they finally told me that the check was less due to the fact that about one-third of the money in the account had been withdrawn a little over three weeks ago and with that amount of principal gone, the income from the account had been reduced. Yes, apparently the Ace Investment account had been transferred into the trust, with April as the trustee, and about three weeks ago she had withdrawn $500,000 from my Ace Investment account. I asked the representative how that was possible. He said that it was possible and legal, as Mr. Aster had assisted the trustee in the transfer and the transferred funds went into his client trust account. I didn't know where the funds were. Apparently the funds were turned over to April. I understand now that it wasn't just the $500,000 that was removed. Another $250,000 of the Ace Investment account was later removed and now those funds may be completely gone. So it appears that a total of $750,000 is now missing. I am very worried about the money, as I will need that money to live on now and in the future.

I never received a bill for attorney fees from Mr. Aster, but I have learned that April was asked by Mr. Aster to give a statement because he thought that I was going to sue him. Well, he turned out to be right, but I had made no such decision when the statement was given. I have reviewed Exhibit 14, and the signature at the bottom of the page is definitely April's. In that statement April said that she paid the fee and retainer charge of $7,500. I never knew that before.

I have always loved my daughter, and to learn that April had in fact taken the money and gone to Peru with the intention of investing the money in some foreign country was almost more than I could handle. I would never have done such a thing, as my investment in Ace Investments was just what I wanted. Then I learned that she disappeared after scuba diving and supposedly there was no sign of her. This has been devastating. I have lost my daughter. I have lost most of my life savings. And I know that Mr. Aster has been behind all of this. After learning the details in Exhibits 10 and 11 of how April disappeared I now believe that there was foul play. I learned that the authorities in Peru suspected that Mr. Aster may have been involved in her disappearance. Through my lawyer I have contacted authorities in Peru and tried to urge them to prosecute Mr. Aster. They claim that they don't have sufficient evidence, but the police say if they do receive any more evidence, they will forward it to the prosecution office. My lawyer has told me that there is a possibility that in this lawsuit we may be able to prove that Mark Aster arranged for April's disappearance to show motive for his taking the money.

Apparently no one can prove that there were any documents signed by April, as I understand they never recovered any such documents in Peru. If so, Mark Aster is not only a greedy thief, he is an evil murderer. He took my only daughter away from me. Exhibit 18 is my daughter's photo. (Witness weeps. A fifteen minute interruption followed allowing Rose Huntington to recover.) I am not normally a mean-spirited person, but I hope that Mark Aster rots in hell. His orchestration of all this is the work of Satan. I hope there is some justice in our court system, and I hope that Mark Aster is never allowed to harm other people like he has so severely harmed our family.

I, ROSE HUNTINGTON, do certify that I have read the foregoing pages of my testimony as transcribed and that it is a true and correct transcript of the testimony given by me in this deposition on August 14, YR-2, in the offices of plaintiff's counsel.

Rose Huntington

Certified by:

Maria de los Ramos
Certified Shorthand Reporter

Deposition of Pat Hardesty

PAT HARDESTY, called to testify on deposition by the defendant and having been fully informed of all rights and obligations and duly sworn, testified as follows (objections omitted):

My name is Pat Hardesty. I am an attorney at law licensed to practice in the State of Nita. I have been admitted to practice for twenty-three years. I am certified by the State Bar of Nita as a specialist in estate planning. In order to be certified in estate planning, I took extensive specialized courses in estate planning and successfully completed the certification exam, which was administered by the State Bar of Nita. I have been a certified specialist in estate planning for ten years. My law practice is in Nita City, Nita, where I am a partner in the law firm of Baker & Wilson. I handle virtually all of the estate planning cases that come into the practice. Not only do I prepare testamentary documents such as wills and trusts, but I also handle all litigation in the firm relative to estate planning matters.

In my practice, I have prepared hundreds of wills and trusts and have handled all types of litigation relative to this area of practice. I have extensive teaching experience in my areas of specialization. For the last six years I have taught Estate Planning, Trust and Wills at the Nita University School of Law. I have also taught continuing education classes in estate planning for lawyers through the Nita State Bar Association Continuing Legal Education Program for the last seven years. My scholarly publication work has revolved around estate planning and professional responsibility. In fact, one of my articles, which was published in the Nita State Bar Journal, dealt in part with issues raised in this case. The article, entitled "Changing Nature of the Family: The Future of Estate Planning" covered not only the changing nature of families over the last several decades, but also the changing nature of tax laws, professional responsibility and liability, and the growing progression of utilizing trusts over wills. The article cited both the advantages of a trust over a will, and the potential dangers of limiting the control of the trust by the trustor. Those dangers erupt in several ways in this case.

In recent years beginning in YR-8 I have served as an expert in cases dealing with my specialized area of practice both in state and federal courts. In total, I have been retained as an expert approximately twenty times, and twelve such cases required my attendance in hearings and trials in both state and federal courts. On each occasion I was found qualified to give expert testimony in my field of practice. I have not limited my service to just one side in such litigations. On eight such cases I testified for the plaintiff, and on four I was retained and testified for the defense.

In preparation for my review and opinions in this case I have examined The Rose Huntington Irrevocable Trust, Exhibit 1; the financial documents marked Exhibits 2 through 7; the two news articles marked Exhibits 10 and 11; the two disciplinary hearing reports marked Exhibits 12 and 13; the statement of April Huntington, marked Exhibit 14; Exhibit 15; the CV of Ashley Price; and Exhibit 17, the Peruvian police report. Also, at counsel's request,

I have reviewed the transcripts of the testimony of Mark Aster, Ashley Price, and Harry Zoldak. I do not personally know anyone related to the present case.

After reviewing the information provided and performing additional research, I have the following observations. This trust is a basic trust, which is usually used by attorneys for clients who would like to have a basic trust for what may be termed "general use." It does not contain overly complicated provisions, and does not attempt to handle unique or specialized issues. One might call it a "boilerplate trust." As Mr. Aster testified in his deposition, the attorney essentially buys software that prepares the trust, nowadays generally on a CD-ROM. He uses that for the basic provisions of the trust, and edits and adds provisions as deemed necessary. Having said that, of course the attorney is always responsible for the final product.

On review, I did not see anything unique or particularly challenging about this trust. What I did note is that some decisions were made as to several provisions, mostly where the proposed terms must be edited to fit the client's situation. I believe that there are several issues that prompted such editing. In analyzing these issues, I have the following thoughts.

In naming the trustee, great care must be taken. When selecting a trustee, the ideal situation is to set up the trust where the trustor, the one whose trust it is, acts as one's own trustee during her lifetime. This allows one to in essence keep control of one's assets during her lifetime. If the trustor is competent, why shouldn't that person manage her own estate? I saw nothing in the records I reviewed that suggested that Mrs. Huntington was not capable of handling her own affairs, both before and after the trust was signed. If she were not so competent, that would suggest that she was not competent to make the disposition of her estate plans at all – that a conservator should have been appointed. But as I say, she gave all signs of being completely *compos mentis*. I will address the issue of her supposed medical condition when get to irrevocable nature of the trust.

If a third party is to be installed as the trustee, it should be one that is impartial. This means that the person selected should be someone who is not beneficially interested in the trust. Generally speaking, an ultimate beneficiary may not be the best choice, as there exists a potential conflict of interest. I should add, however, that it is permissible to have an ultimate beneficiary as trustee.

I am a firm believer that a trustee, other than the trustor acting as a trustee, should be bonded. It is a protection from malfeasance for the estate assets. The cost for such a bond can be high, but the protection to the trust assets is worth the cost.

A "trust protector" is someone nominated by the trust to oversee and protect the trust. This may be particularly useful with a non-professional trustee. This may be proper and appropriate in some cases. As a lawyer, I personally do not seek to have myself so appointed. Unless there is full disclosure, I think there's a conflict of interest. More personally, I don't want to be in a position where I have to try to monitor the independent trustee and possibly assume some liability for the actions of the trustee.

I have been advised that shortly after the checks were issued from Mr. Aster's client trust account to April as trustee, Mr. Aster abruptly resigned as trust protector. I believe that it was appropriate, under the law, for Mr. Aster to resign, the effect of which would be to remove him from further fiduciary responsibilities as a trust protector to the trust. However, I do have some doubts about the propriety of Mr. Aster so removing himself as trust protector at a time when trust assets were in the process of being invested by the trustee in alternative investments.

In my opinion, I would not have sought to have a beneficiary appointed as trustee. I would quite possibly have had Rose act as her own trustee during her lifetime. I would have required a bond for an independent trustee. And, I wouldn't have sought to have myself appointed as the "trust protector."

In my review of the subject trust, it is apparent that this trust is what is called an "irrevocable trust." Irrevocable trusts are most commonly utilized in situations where there is an attempt to shelter assets from the trustor's creditors. The trustor retains no right, title or interest in the principal or income from the trust. All power is thus vested in the trustee. Accordingly, creditors of the trustor are not able to reach the assets that have been transferred into the irrevocable trust.

Normally, there would be no reason to make a trust irrevocable unless there was a situation where substantial debt was anticipated. Once a trust is set up as irrevocable, it cannot be revoked by the trustor. The trustor thus will have given up substantial rights and cannot back out of the deal, so to speak. An irrevocable trust should not be taken lightly, and should only be used in cases where substantial debt is anticipated.

Assuming that Rose Huntington did not anticipate incurring substantial debt, I can see no persuasive reason to set this trust up as being irrevocable. Remember that being irrevocable means that she gives up all power to revoke the trust, or to have any say in the administration of the trust. I see absolutely no evidence in this case that Rose Huntington was likely to incur any substantial debt. The history that I have reviewed suggests the opposite. I have been advised that Rose Huntington had essentially no creditors and did not anticipate having creditors in the foreseeable future. She had substantial funds that in all likelihood would have provided a stable lifetime income, and it would serve no purpose for her to forego controlling those funds in the future. Keep in mind that the trustee of an irrevocable trust has certain fiduciary duties to the trust and its beneficiaries, but all power is essentially removed from the trustor. Perhaps she might have had some diminishing cogency as her age increased, but that could have been dealt with at that time. In my opinion, from the facts as I know them, I would not have drafted this trust to be irrevocable.

I also reviewed Rose's earlier will which was prepared by Seth Middleton and revoked by the subsequent trust. The will met all of the requirements of the Nita probate statutes and was valid in all respects. The only reason that I would have superseded the will with a trust would be to avoid probate expenses, as trusts are not subject to probate and thus costs are reduced substantially.

Having stated my views about The Rose Huntington Trust document and the will, I would like to turn to other information that I have reviewed and considered in expressing my opinion in this case. I have learned that the defendant concedes that he was in a romantic relationship with the trustee, April Huntington. Also, I have been shown Exhibits 12 and 13, the records of Nita State Bar disciplinary proceeding against Mr. Aster. The Nita Rules of Professional Conduct clearly deal with three potential issues raised in this case.

The first deals with sexual relations with clients and very clearly states that such conduct is unprofessional. It is true that April Huntington was not by strict terms "a client," but as a beneficiary and the sole trustee, she was an essential party to the handling of the trust. It is also true that the rule does not apply to sexual relations that predate the initiation of the lawyer-client relationship. And, yes, there may be some evidence in this case that the romantic relationship between April and the defendant predated the defendant's representation of Rose Huntington.

The second deals with the fact that the attorney shall not accept compensation for representing a client from one other than the client. In this case it appears that April bestowed benefits to the defendant beyond that he received in romance. It appears that April paid for not one, but three trips to resort areas, and much of what they did was beyond conferences and negotiations concerning investments, if any such negotiations were ever in fact held.

Another concern is the ethical responsibility that an attorney shall not enter into a business transaction with a client; or knowingly acquire an ownership, possessory, security, or other pecuniary interest adverse to a client. There is a serious question in this case whether assisting April, a beneficiary, in using Rose's funds constitutes such an adverse interest. At the very least, the defendant had an affirmative duty to fully disclose all this to Rose, and according to the information I have, he did not.

It is apparent from my review of disciplinary rulings by the Nita State Bar Association in Exhibits 12 and 13 that the defendant has either had difficulty understanding his legal responsibilities, or has chosen to ignore them.

I believe that the defendant has acted improperly and unprofessionally in the areas I have discussed. I wish I could say otherwise, but the record leaves me no choice. As I said earlier, I have reviewed the testimony of Ashley Price and the opinion given. Obviously, I disagree with that opinion. I certainly acknowledge and respect Ashley Price as an estate planning, probate and trust attorney, but I cannot agree in any way with the conclusion Ashley Price has rendered in this case.

In light of all the concerns I have expressed, it is my opinion, to a reasonable degree of legal certainty, that defendant Mark Aster conducted his representation of Mrs. Huntington's interests measurably short of the standard of care we expect of attorneys practicing in Nita.

I, PAT HARDESTY, do certify that I have read the foregoing pages of my testimony as transcribed and that it is a true and correct transcript of the testimony given by me in this deposition on August 10, YR-2, in the offices of defendant's counsel.

Pat Hardesty

Certified by:

Maria de los Ramos
Certified Shorthand Reporter

I, TAL HURLBERT, do certify that I have read the foregoing pages of my testimony as transcribed and that it is a true and correct transcript of the [illegible] by me in this deposition on August [illegible], in the offices of defendants' counsel.

[illegible]

[illegible]

[illegible]

[illegible]

Deposition of Courtney Brown

COURTNEY BROWN, called to testify on deposition by the defendant and having been fully informed of all rights and obligations and duly sworn, testified as follows (objections omitted):

My name is Courtney Brown. I am a real estate agent and a notary public. I have lived in Greenville all of my life. Greenville is a small town and I have come to know most everyone in town. I work in a real estate office at 180 Main Street, which is just up the street from Mark Aster's new law office. He recently moved to town and, in passing, we have gotten to know each other.

On the day that Rose Huntington signed her trust, Mark requested that I come to his office at 10:00 a.m., about the same time that she arrived for her appointment. I arrived at about 10:00 a.m., just as Mark, Rose and April were going into his office. I expected to wait in the waiting room until it was time to sign the document; however, Mark asked me to come right in with all of them. So I went on in. Being a lifelong resident of Greenville, I know Rose Huntington and in fact, I had gone to high school with her daughter April. That being the case, the whole situation was a bit uncomfortable. I went in and sat down quietly, as I didn't think that I should say anything as this was Mark's office and I was being employed by him to notarize the document.

After a few niceties, Mark got out the trust and tried to summarize it for Rose. It appeared to be many pages and Rose apparently did not want to read it in its entirety. From the outset of the appointment, I got the impression that the matter of this trust was Mark and April's idea, and that Rose was basically there to sign. I didn't pay a lot of attention to Mark's summary of the document as I thought it was personal. I do remember hearing that April would be the trustee, no bond would be required, and all three children, Warren, John, and April, would be the beneficiaries. There was no detailed discussion of the trust and its many pages.

I do remember some discussion about who would be the trustee. Rose said something like, "Why isn't Warren the trustee?" and Mark said something about how Warren wasn't nearby and April would be close and available to her at all times and would be able to discuss how she was handling the trust. Rose mentioned that she never had any problem dealing with Warren on the will where he was the executor. It didn't seem to me at the time that Rose was feeling quite the same as April and Mark. I also noted throughout the whole process that April and Mark constantly looked at each other, in other words, were making eye contact, especially when Rose was looking at the document.

I recall that about forty minutes into the meeting April said something like, "Okay, Mom, why don't you just go ahead and sign so that we can get on with our day." At that point, Mark set out the signature page to Rose for her signature. Whereupon, she signed on the line and I followed up with my notary procedures. As I left, I remember thinking to myself that I was surprised how the whole matter was very summary in nature, and that I'm not sure that Rose understood what was transpiring. Please understand, though, that I am not a lawyer and all I know about this is from that one encounter in Mark's office. Yes, Exhibit 1 is the trust document that I am referring to, and it appears to be in the same condition that it was the day that I notarized it.

As I said earlier, I had known April for a number of years. I bumped into her at the Lucky Market several weeks later, and I asked her how the trust was working out. She said she hoped it would be okay, but she wasn't sure that Mark was going to let her handle the estate. She used the words "pretty controlling" to describe Mark. I think I mentioned something to her about how Mark is a lawyer and he must know what he is talking about. That was the last time I talked to April. Yes, Exhibit 18 is a photo of April. I understand it is her driver's license photo.

I have been told that the reason I am giving this deposition is that April disappeared under suspicious circumstances in South America, and Rose is suing Mark over the trust. I don't really favor either side, but I have to say that I am extremely concerned about what happened to April. As I understand it, a substantial amount of Rose's money that was in the trust is gone, and Rose won't have enough money to support herself in her later years. When I learned of all this, it made me very sad. It is all so tragic.

I, COURTNEY BROWN, do certify that I have read the foregoing pages of my testimony as transcribed and that it is a true and correct transcript of the testimony given by me in this deposition on August 24, YR-2, in the office of defendant's counsel.

Courtney Brown

Courtney Brown

Certified by:

Maria de los Ramos

Maria de los Ramos
Certified Shorthand Reporter

Exhibit 1

THE ROSE HUNTINGTON IRREVOCABLE TRUST

Mark Aster
SPECIALIST IN ESTATE PLANNING, WILLS, TRUSTS,
AND PROBATE ADMINISTRATION
100 Main Street
Greenville, Nita

THE ROSE HUNTINGTON IRREVOCABLE TRUST

The parties to this Trust are ROSE HUNTINGTON (the "Trustor"), and APRIL HUNTINGTON (the "Trustee").

By this agreement, it is intended to create a valid trust under the laws of the State of Nita and under the laws of any state in which this Trust is administered.

The Trustor may not serve as Trustee of any trust created under this agreement at any time.

Section 1.0 Identity of the Trust

This trust when executed shall be known as the "THE ROSE HUNTINGTON IRREVOCABLE TRUST."

Section 1.1 Reliance by Third Parties

No person or entity doing business with the Trustee shall be required to verify the terms of this agreement or the authority of the Trustee, or to inquire into the authority of the Trustee as to any transaction.

Section 1.2 Irrevocable Trust

This Trust is irrevocable, and cannot be altered, amended, revoked, or terminated in any way.

Section 1.3 Transfers to the Trust

Transferred to the Trustee is the following property: residence, timber land, and the Ace Investment account, to be held on the terms and conditions set forth in this instrument. I retain no right, title, or interest in the income or principal of this trust or any other property interest in any trust property.

The Trustee shall hold the above described trust property. The Trustee will administer all trust property for the benefit of my beneficiaries in accordance with the terms of this agreement.

Section 1.4 Statement of Intent

This trust and the assets therein shall be held for the benefit of the trust beneficiaries on the terms and conditions set forth in this agreement. In order to maximize the benefit to my trust beneficiaries, I give the Trustee broad discretion with respect to the management and investment of assets in the trust. One of my specific objectives in creating this trust is preserving my assets so that this trust shall not be subject to the claims of any of my creditors or to any beneficiary's creditors.

All provisions of this trust shall be construed so as to accomplish the above objective. Any beneficiary has the right at any time to disclaim any right or interest that might be construed or deemed to defeat these objectives.

Section 2.0 Trustee Removal by Trust Protector

At any time during my life, the Trust Protector may remove without cause or appoint a Trustee.

Section 3.0 Duties of Trust Protector

The duty of the Trust Protector is to direct the Trustee in matters concerning the trust, and to assist, if needed, in achieving my objectives as manifested by the other provisions of my estate plan. The Trust Protector must be an individual who is not related to any beneficiary.

Section 3.1 Designation of Trust Protector

I hereby appoint the attorney who drafted this trust to serve as Trust Protector of this trust.

Section 3.2 Removal and Replacement of Trust Protector

The Trust Protector may be removed only for cause, subject to the terms of this Trust, as determined by a court which may be initiated by the petition of the Trustor, the Trustee, or any beneficiary. A court removing a Trust Protector may appoint a successor Trust Protector.

Section 3.3 Trust Protector Liability

The Trust Protector is not liable for any action in the absence of a showing, by clear and convincing evidence, that the action taken was carried out with willful neglect, willful misconduct, or is shown by clear and convincing evidence to have been performed in bad faith. The Trust Protector may be liable if it is conclusively established that any act or omission was motivated by an actual intent to harm the trust, or was an act of self-dealing for personal pecuniary benefit.

The Trust Protector shall be indemnified and held harmless from any loss, claim, or damage incurred as a result of any action taken against the Trust Protector.

Section 3.4 Trust Protector Authority

a) The Trust Protector has the Authority to Amend or Modify the Trust Agreement

The Trust Protector may amend or modify this agreement.

An amendment or modification by the Trust Protector shall be binding and conclusive on all persons, unless the amendment is made by willful neglect, willful misconduct, or bad faith shown by clear and convincing evidence. The Trust Protector shall not be liable for any consequences of amending or not amending the trust.

b) Power to Add or Remove Trustor as a Discretionary Beneficiary

The Trust Protector may add the Trustor as a lifetime beneficiary of this trust on a purely discretionary basis and not with any mandatory or ascertainable distribution right. The Trust Protector may only add Trustor if the Trust Protector determines that doing so will not cause the assets of the trust to become subject to the claims of any of creditors.

The Trust Protector may thereafter remove Trustor as beneficiary or otherwise modify any interest granted to Trustor under the trust.

c) **Power to Construe the Terms of this Agreement**

The Trust Protector is to ensure that the trust agreement is consistent with my estate planning objectives.

d) **Power to Resign**

The Trust Protector may resign at any time at his sole discretion.

Section 3.5 Trust Protector Powers

The Trust Protector may not exercise any power for the Trust Protector's benefit, or for the benefit of any person related to the Trust Protector.

Section 3.6 Trust Protector Compensation

The Trust Protector is entitled to receive reasonable compensation for services to the trust. The Trust Protector may receive reimbursement for all expenses incurred in relation to the trust, including reasonable travel expenses.

The Trust Protector may also provide legal and investment advice on behalf of the trust or the trust beneficiaries.

Section 3.7 Inspection of Trust Records

The records of the trust must be open and available for inspection by the Trust Protector and the Trustee at all reasonable times.

Section 3.8 No Judicial Intervention

The trust shall be administered consistent with the provisions of the trust without the approval or action of any court.

Section 3.9 Bond is Waived

The Trustee is not required to furnish any bond whatsoever.

A Trustee of this trust will not be liable to the trust, nor to any trust beneficiary, for any act or decision if the Trustee did not realize an economic benefit or personal gain from the transaction, unless the Trustee acted in bad faith or was grossly negligent.

A Trustee is not liable for any loss to the trust or to the trust beneficiaries for any investment of the trust property in a partnership, limited partnership, limited liability company, or other entity.

Section 4.0 Compensation of Trustee

A Trustee is entitled to fair and reasonable compensation for the services rendered to the trust.

Section 4.1 Trust Accounting

The Trustee is not required to file accountings.

Section 5.0 Trustee's Powers

Except as otherwise specifically provided in this agreement, the Trustee may exercise the powers conferred by this Trust without prior approval from any court.

The Trustee shall exercise the Trustee's powers in the manner the Trustee determines to be in the best interests of the beneficiaries.

Section 5.1 Execution of Documents

The Trustee may execute all instruments in writing that the Trustee considers necessary to carry out any of the powers granted in this Trust.

Section 5.2 Investments of Trust funds

The Trustee may invest in any type of investment, whether inside or outside of the United States of America.

The Trustee may acquire and retain investments not regarded as traditional or suitable assets for trusts, including investments that would be forbidden or would be regarded as imprudent, improper, or unlawful by the "prudent person" rule, "prudent investor" rule, or any other rule or law that restricts a fiduciary's investment plan. The Trustee may invest in any type of property, wherever located, improved or unimproved real property, and personal property, and in any manner, including direct purchase, joint ventures, partnerships, limited partnerships, limited liability companies, corporations, mutual funds, or any other form of ownership.

Section 5.3 Securities

The Trustee may buy, sell, or trade stocks, bonds, mutual funds, or other securities of any kind and in any amount.

Section 6.0 Spendthrift Provision

Neither the income nor the principal of this Trust may be assigned, encumbered, alienated, or otherwise involuntarily transferred in any manner or by any means whatsoever. Neither the income nor the principal of this trust is subject to levy, attachment, federal court proceedings including bankruptcy proceedings, state court proceedings, or any other legal process, subject to the control of creditors or any other person or entity.

Section 7.0 Residual Beneficiaries

Upon Trustor's demise, the remaining trust assets shall be distributed in equal shares to Trustor's son WARREN HUNTINGTON, Trustor's son JOHN HUNTINGTON, and Trustor's daughter APRIL HUNTINGTON.

I have executed this agreement on the day and year first above written. I understand that this irrevocable trust shall be effective when signed.

Rose Huntington, Trustor

ROSE HUNTINGTON, Trustor

April Huntington, Trustee

APRIL HUNTINGTON, Trustee

State of NITA,)
)
County of DARROW)

On *November 7, YR-3* before me, COURTNEY BROWN, a Notary Public, personally appeared ROSE HUNTINGTON, who proved to me on the basis of satisfactory evidence to be the person whose name is subscribed to the within instrument and acknowledged to me that she executed the same in her authorized capacity, and that by her signature on the instrument the person, or the entity upon behalf of which the person acted, executed the instrument.

I certify under penalty of perjury under the laws of the State of Nita that the foregoing paragraph is true and correct.

WITNESS my hand and official seal.

Courtney Brown
COURTNEY BROWN

State of NITA,)
)
County of DARROW)

On *November 7, YR-3* before me, COURTNEY BROWN, a Notary Public, personally appeared APRIL HUNTINGTON, who proved to me on the basis of satisfactory evidence to be the person whose name is subscribed to the within instrument and acknowledged to me that she executed the same in her authorized capacity, and that by her signature on the instrument the person, or the entity upon behalf of which the person acted, executed the instrument.

I certify under penalty of perjury under the laws of the State of Nita that the foregoing paragraph is true and correct.

WITNESS my hand and official seal.

Courtney Brown
COURTNEY BROWN

Exhibit 2

ACE INVESTMENTS ACCOUNT
$500,000 CHECK

supercheck.net

Ace Investment Account
for The Rose Huntington Irrevocable Trust
P. O. Box 77492, Greenville, Nita 85521

145

December 20, Yr-3
DATE

PAY TO THE ORDER OF Mark Aster, Attorney Client Trust Acct $ 500,000.00

Five Hundred Thousand and no/100 ---------------- DOLLARS

Contains Security Features. Details on Back.

Nita National Bank
349 Commerce Drive
Greenville, Nita 85525

WARNING!
DO NOT ACCEPT THIS CHECK UNLESS YOU CAN SEE A TRUE WATERMARK WHEN HOLDING THE CHECK TO THE LIGHT AND ON REVERSE SIDE PINK LOCK AND KEY ICONS THAT CHANGE COLOR WHEN WARMED

MEMO Change of investments

April Huntington, Trustee MP

⑆000067894⑆ 12345678⑈ 0145

Exhibit 3

ACE INVESTMENTS ACCOUNT
$250,000 CHECK

Ace Investment Account
for The Rose Huntington Irrevocable Trust
P. O. Box 77492, Greenville, Nita 85521

146

December 30, Yr-3
DATE

PAY TO THE ORDER OF Mark Aster, Attorney Client Trust Acct. $ 250,000.00

Two Hundred and Fifty Thousand and no/100 DOLLARS Contains Security Features. Details on Back.

Nita National Bank
349 Commerce Drive
Greenville, Nita 85525

WARNING!
DO NOT ACCEPT THIS CHECK UNLESS YOU CAN SEE A TRUE WATERMARK WHEN HOLDING THE CHECK TO THE LIGHT AND ON REVERSE SIDE PINK LOCK AND KEY ICONS THAT CHANGE COLOR WHEN WARMED

MEMO Change of investments

April Huntington, Trustee MP

⑆000067894⑆ 12345678⑈ 0146

Exhibit 4

ASTER ATTORNEY CLIENT CHECK #112

THE FACE OF THIS DOCUMENT HAS A BLUE CHECK BACKGROUND ON WHITE PAPER AND A VOID PANTOGRAPH WITH A BLUE SECURITY STRIP IN CENTER

Mark Aster, Attorney Client Trust Account
for April Huntington
6225 Downton Avenue
Greenville, Nita 85522
(555) 365-6078

11-24/1210(8)

No. 112
Date: *Jan. 2, YR-2*

Pay to the Order of *April Huntington, Trustee of the Rose Huntington Irrevocable Trust* | *$500,000.00*

Security features included. Details on back.

the sum of Five Hundred Thousand and no/100 dollars

Signed *Mark Aster*

⑈0150482880⑈ ⑆121000248⑆ 4861 507112

Exhibit 5

ASTER ATTORNEY CLIENT CHECK #115

THE FACE OF THIS DOCUMENT HAS A BLUE CHECK BACKGROUND ON WHITE PAPER AND A VOID PANTOGRAPH WITH A BLUE SECURITY STRIP IN CENTER

Mark Aster, Attorney Client Trust Account
for April Huntington
6225 Downton Avenue
Greenville, Nita 85522
(555) 365-6078

11-24/1210(8)

No. 115
Date: Jan. 15, YR-2

Pay to the Order of April Huntington, Trustee of the Rose Huntington Irrevocable Trust, the sum of Two Hundred and Fifty Thousand and no/100 dollars

$250,000.00

Security features included. Details on back.

Signed Mark Aster

⑈015048 2880⑈ ⑆121000248⑆ 4861 507115

Exhibit 6

ELECTRONIC TRANSFER

REQUEST FOR ELECTRONIC TRANSFER OF FUNDS

To: NITA NATIONAL BANK, Greenville, Nita

Account: The Rose Huntington Irrevocable Trust

Account Number: 4861-804000

Requestor: APRIL HUNTINGTON, TRUSTEE OF THE ROSE HUNTINGTON IRREVOCABLE TRUST.

Date: February 11, YR-2

It is hereby requested that the following funds be withdrawn from the above-referenced account:

Date of Withdrawal: February 12, YR-2

Amount of Withdrawal: $500,000.00 [Five Hundred Thousand Dollars]

Recipient Bank: Banco de la Nacion, Mancora, Peru

Recipient Account:

- Routing Number: 99575-3328
- Account Number: 066-559-4412

I, April Huntington, Trustee of The Rose Huntington Irrevocable Trust, **hereby request and authorize the above referenced electronic transfer.**

April Huntington

April Huntington, Trustee of
The Rose Huntington Irrevocable Trust

Exhibit 7

ELECTRONIC TRANSFER

REQUEST FOR ELECTRONIC TRANSFER OF FUNDS

To: NITA NATIONAL BANK, Greenville, Nita

Account: The Rose Huntington Irrevocable Trust

Account Number: 4861-804000

Requestor: APRIL HUNTINGTON, TRUSTEE OF THE ROSE HUNTINGTON IRREVOCABLE TRUST.

Date: February 11, YR-2

It is hereby requested that the following funds be withdrawn from the above-referenced account:

Date of Withdrawal: February 12, YR-2

Amount of Withdrawal: $250,000.00 [Two Hundred and Fifty Thousand Dollars]

Recipient Bank: Banco de la Nacion, Mancora, Peru

Recipient Account:

- Routing Number: 99575-3328
- Account Number: 066-559-4420

I, April Huntington, Trustee of The Rose Huntington Irrevocable Trust, **hereby request and authorize the above referenced electronic transfer.**

April Huntington

April Huntington, Trustee of
The Rose Huntington Irrevocable Trust

Exhibit 8

PHOTO OF APRIL SCUBA DIVING

Exhibit 9

PAINTING OF LA COSTA MAGNIFICA

Exhibit 10

NEWS RELEASE

La Noticia de Mancora

March 8, YR –2	**English Edition**

POLICE INVESTIGATE MYSTERIOUS DISAPPEARANCE

By Estellia Mercado

LA COSTA MAGNIFICA - Police are seeking potential witnesses who could provide information concerning the recent disappearance on March 6th of an American tourist who disappeared after scuba diving of the coast.

Police Chief Ernesto Diego said that police and lifeguards searched for thirty-six-year-old April Huntington after she disappeared either while or shortly after scuba diving. She was described as an American financier who was investing in the new resort of La Costa Magnifica, located near Mancora and Punta Sal. Chief Diego announced that she was diving with her companion, Mark Aster, a lawyer from the State of Nita, United States. According to Aster, the two were on a business trip in connection with both the resort at La Costa Magnifica and the Peruvian Land and Mining Company.

Aster told police that the two went scuba diving about 1:30 p.m., departing from the launch point near the La Costa Magnifica landing. Aster said that they had been diving, and they separated with Huntington diving in an area of rocks and caves. Aster said that they were to join in one area, and when he went to the meeting spot, Huntington was gone. Aster said that he frantically tried to find her, but she was nowhere to be found.

Aster said he immediately returned to the coast and called for help. Lifeguards in the area searched and could find no sign of her. According to lifeguard Emilio Sanchez, there was no clothing, equipment, or any other evidence indicating that Huntington died at the scene.

A member of Chief Diego's office privately expressed some skepticism about her disappearance, and said that all efforts to locate her or to find evidence of her departure from La Costa Magnifica proved fruitless. Police found no evidence of a struggle. Police officials are trying to determine if Aster had any motive to kill Huntington. Witnesses including visitors and employees at La Costa Magnifica all stated that they saw no sign of conflict between the two, and they appeared to be happily enjoying their stay and each other's company.

Officials of the Greenville Police Department in the State of Nita, U.S.A. said they were unaware of the disappearance of Huntington, and they had not received such information.

The Security Offices of La Costa Magnifica and the Peruvian Land and Mining were both unavailable for comment.

Exhibit 11

NEWS RELEASE

La Noticia de Mancora

March 17, YR –2 **English Edition**

POLICE CONTINUE THEIR INVESTIGATION INTO MYSTERIOUS DISAPPEARANCE

By Estellia Mercado

LA COSTA MAGNIFICA- Police continue to follow up on their investigation of the recent March 6th disappearance of American tourist and financier April Huntington, who disappeared after scuba diving off the coast. The police are checking claims made by attorney Mark Aster, Huntington's companion, that an elaborate conspiracy to steal nearly a million American dollars from Huntington was perpetrated by unknown individuals. Police have looked into these accusations and so far have found no evidence to corroborate Aster's claims.

Police Chief Ernesto Diego said that his agency has spoken with agents of La Costa Magnifica and The Peruvian Land and Mining Company and can find no evidence that those agencies have ever been contacted by either Aster or Huntington. Also, they have checked with Banco de la Nacion and the only record shows Huntington receiving $750,000 in American money on February 12th of this year, and that receipt was signed by one witness, Mark Aster.

Chief Diego said that Aster claimed that extensive negotiations were conducted not only with representatives of La Costa and the Peruvian Land and Mining Co., but also with an agent of the national government. Chief Diego's agency has been unable to confirm any of these claims. In fact, Chief Diego said that they were totally unable to locate or identify any of the individuals whose names were given by Aster. Chief Diego said that his agency and the two businesses as well as the national government would be greatly concerned if any such criminal conspiracy were at work.

Chief Diego also said that Aster claimed that the invested funds were insured by the national government. According to their investigation, there is no government program that would insure such investment funds unless the United States government would do so.

Chief Diego further expressed the frustration of not being able to determine the exact cause of April Huntington's disappearance. Police officers were unable to locate any of the alleged documents in this case. Chief Diego has contacted the Greenville Police Department in the United States, and asked them to send his department any further information they develop.

He said that the only kidnappings of Americans have been in Cusco and Machu Picchu, and he was unaware of any in the coastal region of Peru. His department has circulated a photo of April Huntington to all police offices in the nation. He said that should any further information be received, they would reopen their review of the case. Otherwise, it will remain a missing persons report.

Exhibit 12

NITA STATE BAR DISPOSITION YR-6

STATE BAR OF NITA

HEARING DEPARTMENT – NITA CITY

In the Matter of **MARK ALLEN ASTER** **Member No. 94161** A Member of the State Bar	Case No.: **YR-6-2,071** **STIPULATION RE FACTS, CONCLUSIONS OF LAW AND DISPOSITION**

FACTS AND CONCLUSIONS OF LAW

I.

1. On or about October 13, YR-7, Perry Currin employed respondent to prepare a revocable trust instrument and transfer Currin's property into the trust on an expedited basis. Currin paid respondent $1,250.00 for this service. Currin's home was a primary piece of property to be transferred into the trust.
2. Thereafter, respondent failed to promptly transfer Currin's home into the trust.
3. On several occasions, including on or about January 21, YR-6, February 27, YR-6, March 9, YR-6, and August 14, YR-6, Currin left messages asking respondent to provide Currin with information regarding the status of his request that his home be transferred into the trust and to otherwise contact him regarding this matter.
4. By, on, or about May 28, YR-6, the State Bar was conducting an inquiry and investigation into a complaint filed by Currin concerning allegations that respondent failed to diligently perform legal services on Currin's behalf in relation to the revocable trust.
5. On or about May 28, YR-6, June 30, YR-6 and September 11, YR-6, the State Bar contacted respondent by letter concerning Currin's complaint; respondent received each of these letters shortly after they were sent to him.
6. Respondent transferred Currin's home into the trust on or about November 24, YR-6. By delaying until on or about November 24, YR-6, to transfer Currin's home into trust, respondent recklessly and repeatedly failed to perform legal services with competence in violation of Rule 3-11(A) of the NITA State Bar Rules of Professional Conduct.

7. By failing to respond to Currin's requests for information about the transfer of his home into the trust or otherwise, respondent failed to respond promptly to reasonable status inquiries of a client in violation of Rule 3-50 of the NITA State Bar Rules of Professional Conduct.

STAYED SUSPENSION ORDER

II.

Stayed Suspension

Respondent must be suspended from the practice of law for a period of ONE (1) YEAR. The above-referenced suspension is stayed.

Probation

Respondent is placed on probation for a period of TWO (2) YEARS, which will commence upon the effective date of this order.

Conditions of Probation

1. Respondent must comply with the provisions of the Nita State Bar Act and the Nita Rules of Professional Conduct.
2. Within thirty (30) days, respondent must contact the Nita State Bar Office of Probation to discuss these terms and must promptly meet with the probation deputy as directed and upon request.
3. Respondent must submit written quarterly reports to the Nita State Bar Office of Probation each January 10, April 10, July 10, and October 10 of the period of probation. Respondent, under penalty of perjury, must state that respondent has complied with all conditions of probation.
4. Within one (1) year of the effective date of this order, respondent must provide the Nita State Bar Office of Probation satisfactory proof of attendance at a session of the Nita State Bar Ethics School, and passage of the test given at the end of the session.
5. Respondent must provide proof of passage of the Multistate Professional Responsibility Examination administered by the National Conference of Bar Examiners to the Nita State Bar Office of Probation within one (1) year.

Order

Finding the stipulation to be fair to the parties and that it adequately protects the public, IT IS ORDERED that the requested dismissal of counts/charges is GRANTED without prejudice, and:

The stipulated facts and disposition are APPROVED and the DISCIPLINE RECOMMENDED to the Nita Supreme Court. All hearing dates are vacated. The parties are bound by the stipulation.

Date: June 10, YR-5 Warren Brown State Bar Court Judge

Date: June 10, YR-5 Mark Aster Respondent

Exhibit 13

NITA STATE BAR DISPOSITION YR-3

STATE BAR OF NITA

HEARING DEPARTMENT – NITA CITY

In the Matter of **MARK ALLEN ASTER** **Member No. 94161** A Member of the State Bar	Case No.: **YR-3-695** **STIPULATION RE FACTS, CONCLUSIONS OF LAW AND DISPOSITION**

FACTS AND CONCLUSIONS OF LAW

I.

1. On or about July 22, YR-4 Elizabeth Judnich hired respondent to represent her in a personal injury matter. On September 19, YR-4, respondent filed an action on her behalf. (*Elizabeth Judnich v. Jerry Witte and the County of Darrow*, Darrow County District Court, case no. PV4974.)
2. On or about November 14, YR-4, Judnich and Jerry Witte executed a stipulated settlement. Respondent received $42,000 on behalf of Judnich.
3. On or about December 6, YR-4, respondent retained $6,000 of the $42,000 for himself as attorney fees, which was approved by Judnich. Respondent placed the remaining $36,000 into a segregated, individual client trust account, entitled Mark Aster & Associates, Inc., Attorney/Client Trust Account, Judnich v. Witte, et al., account number 2605371 at Nita State Bank (hereinafter "Judnich Trust Account").
4. On or about January 14, YR-3, respondent withdrew $5,000 cash from the Judnich Trust Account. Respondent withdrew the funds for his own personal use and not for any purpose on behalf of Judnich.
5. By failing to maintain the full $36,000 in funds in trust on behalf of Judnich and by taking $5,000 for his own purposes, respondent failed to maintain client funds in trust, in willful violation of the NITA State Bar Rules of Professional Conduct, Rule 4-10(A).

AGGRAVATING CIRCUMSTANCES

1. Nita State Bar case no. YR-6-2,071.
2. Degree of prior discipline one (1) year stayed suspension, two (2) years of probation.
3. Trust violation where trust funds and property were involved and respondent did not provide a proper account to Judnich.

MITIGATING CIRCUMSTANCES

1. By March 14, YR-3, respondent had contacted The Nita State Bar Lawyer's Assistance Program ("LAP") and completed the intake process. Respondent signed an evaluation agreement with LAP, whereby he was assessed and monitored for a period of time.
2. Respondent admits that the above facts are true and that he is culpable of violations of the specified section of the Nita Rules of Professional Conduct.
3. When respondent was first contacted by the Nita State Bar on or about February 8, YR-3, respondent immediately withdrew $5,000 from his personal account and replaced that sum in the Judnich Trust Account.
4. Respondent's legal secretary, Geraldine Swartz, verified in a properly notarized document that she had negligently withdrawn the $5,000 from Judnich Trust Account instead of the Mark Aster & Associates, Inc., Attorney/Client Trust Account.

ORDER

By respondent's signature below, respondent signifies his agreement with each of the recitations and each of the terms and conditions of this Stipulation Re. Facts and Conclusions of Law.

Respondent enters into this Stipulation as a condition of his participation in LAP. Respondent understands that he must abide by all terms and conditions of LAP contract.

If respondent is not accepted into LAP or does not sign the LAP contract, this Stipulation will be rejected and will not be binding on respondent or The Nita State Bar.

Upon respondent's successful completion of LAP, the charges filed in this case shall be dismissed without prejudice.

Finding the Stipulation to be fair to the parties and that it adequately protects the public, the stipulated facts and disposition are APPROVED and the DISCIPLINE RECOMMENDED to the Nita Supreme Court. All hearing dates are vacated. The parties are bound by the stipulation.

Date: May 6, YR-3 Kirkham Jott State Bar Court Judge

Date: May 6, YR-3 Mark Aster Respondent

Exhibit 14

STATEMENT OF APRIL HUNTINGTON

My name is April Huntington. I am giving this statement because I have been informed by Mark Aster that there has been an accusation by my mother, Rose Huntington, that Mr. Aster has stolen money from her and has convinced me to assist him. I am thirty-six years old. I am the daughter of Rose and Caspar Huntington. I grew up in Greenville. My father died about ten years ago and until recently, I lived with my mother on and off. I was married to Harry Zoldak for about four years. We lived in Nita City. The whole thing was a mistake. Harry drank too much and never held a job very long. I left him in YR-5. I remained in Nita City. I got a job working as a waitress at Sam's Pancake House for almost two years.

Then I worked handling the phones and running the front desk at Jeff Heath's Chevrolet dealership. That was a big mistake. Jeff and I had sort of an affair. He was married. Sometimes he would ask me to set aside some company money so that we could go on weekend trips out of town. Well, his wife found out about it and also found out he had been hiding money. That's when Jeff turned on me and called the cops and said I was embezzling money. He turned over books he had ordered me to cook, and he apparently ordered the bookkeeper, Billy Hitchcock, to tell the cops that he had discovered the altered books. When I was arrested, I told the cops what had happened and told them where we had gone on our trips, but they never followed up. I didn't want my mother to know and I didn't have any money, so I got a public defender. My lawyer said it didn't matter, since I knew what I was doing, and I had better take a plea and get probation. So that's what I did. I saw Jeff about a year later at a bar, and when he saw me he just laughed and he turned around and left.

It is true that in addition to the embezzlement conviction, I was convicted before that of a bad checks charge. I had a bank account and had been promised a bonus from the company that I worked for and it didn't come through. I ended up owing almost four thousand dollars and some additional bad check expenses. I pled no contest and I paid off every check. My mother was a big help.

Anyway, I moved back home with my mother in Greenville. I was depressed. I started drinking almost every night. I would go to Jason's Tavern. I saw a waitress I used to know when I went to high school. It was around then that I met Mark Aster at Jason's. I was between jobs at the time and I still had some money I had saved. I was interested in finding a stable job and improving myself. I talked some with Mark, who was relatively new in Greenville and was establishing his law practice. I began to see Mark more often, usually at Jason's. He encouraged me to help him in his practice and I began working for him part time. It was exciting. He allowed me to talk with new clients, interview them, and complete a screening file. I began to learn quite a few things about the practice of law. That was especially true about what he called estate planning.

That's when I began to worry about my mother's situation. She had an old and rather simple will and I knew that she had a pretty sizable estate. So I talked with Mark several times about this. Mark became concerned that my mother was risking not only her own money, but also the money she would pass on to her heirs. He mentioned the problem of huge probate fees and tax consequences. I knew enough by then about estate planning to realize that I had better talk to my mother, which I did. I really don't think she had a clue. This will she had was prepared by a family friend and that lawyer never really talked to my mother about any of these concerns. I discussed this several times with her; her usual response was to say that the will had worked fine for my father and it would work fine for her. My father died years ago and there had been many pretty big changes in tax and probate laws. Well, even though my mother became irritated with me for continuing to bring this up, she finally agreed to meet with Mark, and that meeting took place about a week later in Mark's office.

Mark was terrific. He was patient and he did not try to push anything. At the first meeting, he simply wanted to educate my mother on what some of the problems would be if she passed away and her estate went through probate. She kept saying that she would prefer to stay with a will because she controlled the process and she wanted to make sure that her three children would get their fair shares. I did interject several times to mention to her that with my limited experience in the area of estate planning and tax law, I felt this was the best way to accomplish what she was after. Mark asked her to think about it and we scheduled a follow-up meeting in a couple of weeks.

I was still living at home and so we talked every once in awhile about this. She would sometimes get cross with me. She accused me of drinking too much and she even suggested that I was doing this because Mark and I had some kind of affair. That wasn't true. Sure, Mark and I were having a relationship. She said she knew we were going off on weekend trips together. I told her I was not a child anymore and there was nothing sinful about this. She said I was drinking more now that I was spending time with Mark. Well, we had our follow-up meeting and Mark had prepared the trust. He patiently went through the whole document sentence by sentence, explaining every aspect of the trust. Mother did not ask many questions and at the end of the meeting she signed the trust. I told her that since I was the trustee, I would be able to protect her and make sure that her wishes were honored. I know that Mark explained fully the provision that the trust was irrevocable. She never asked any questions or expressed any concern about that. Exhibit 1 appears to be an accurate copy of the trust that Mark prepared for my mother. I didn't want to upset my mother further, so I told Mark that I would pay his $2,500.00 fee, and I paid with a personal check.

I moved out of my mother's home and into an apartment several weeks later. That's when I suggested to Mark that her investment with Ace was a bad one and I should seek a better return for her. Mark was very kind and offered several suggestions. I then decided to have those funds withdrawn and placed in a trust account. Mark did not know this, but part of my thinking was that I had learned a good deal about investments and instead of my mother earning a mere $8,000 a month, we could probably double that through wise investments.

I talked to several people in the investment field and learned of a huge real estate and mining development in South America with headquarters in Lima, Peru. I talked to Mark and we decided to personally visit the area.

First, we flew to Fort Lauderdale, Florida and met with a gentleman named Alfonso Escobar, who was the Executive Vice President of The Peruvian Land and Mining Company. That was only a two-day trip. As a follow up, a week later we flew to a beach resort in Peru called La Costa Magnifica. We met with three officers of the company and we were assured that my mother's assets were fully insured by the Peruvian government by a federal law similar to our FDIC. While we were there, Mark introduced me to scuba diving and we took two dives. My previous scuba diving experience was a junior college class and I really had not done it since. Well, this was an incredible experience. The fellow in charge of scuba diving at the resort gave us a verbal rundown on the use of the equipment and safety tips, and then he took us out away from the resort along the rocks. I saw incredible sea life and we vowed to return and make more dives in the rocks off the coast. When we left, the instructor gave me a photo he took showing me underwater. Mark asked if he could have that and I gave it to him.

I invested $500,000 of the former Ace funds in stock in The Peruvian Land and Mining Company and another $250,000 in the La Costa Magnifica development. We were both assured that the annual return on those investments would amount to over $120,000, plus money that remained in mother's trust. To insure that these investments will continue to be secure, Mark and I will return next month to more closely monitor these funds. There were some expenses as a result of our trips to Ft. Lauderdale and La Costa, around $19,000 in total. My mother is not speaking to me now, but I'm sure that when she begins to receive more income, she'll realize the value of what Mark and I have done for her. I'm sure that her comments about suing Mark are just frustration based on her ignorance of what we have done for her and what the benefits will be.

I have read the above statement, consisting of three pages, and it is true and correct.

Signed: *April Huntington* Date: February 20, YR-2

April Huntington

Witnessed: *Albert Zarilla* Date: February 20, YR-2

Albert Zarilla

Exhibit 15

CURRICULUM VITAE ASHLEY PRICE

ASHLEY PRICE, J.D., MBA
1601 HEFFERNAN DRIVE, SUITE 410
NITA CITY, NITA 99915
(555) 365-6066
(555) 365-6067 (FAX)
ASHLEYPRICE@APRICELAW.COM (E-MAIL)

EDUCATIONAL BACKGROUND

BA, with Great Distinction, Nita State University, YR-15
JD, University of Nita, Nita Law School, Robert Muncrief Three-Year Scholarship, YR-12
MBA, Graziadio School of Business, Pepperdine University, YR-8

EMPLOYMENT HISTORY

Associate Attorney, Law Offices of Berardino and Kinder, Nita City, YR-12 to YR-9
Principal Attorney, Ashley Price Law Offices, YR-9 to Present
Legal Malpractice, Estate Planning, Probate, and Trust Law Expert, YR-6 to Present

CERTIFICATION AND LICENSURE

Admitted to Practice in All Nita Courts - November, YR-12
Admitted to Practice in Central District of Nita Federal Court, YR-12
Certified Specialist, Estate Planning, Probate, and Trust Law, Nita State Bar, YR-6
Certified Specialist, Elder Law, Nita State Bar, YR-4

PROFESSIONAL ASSOCIATIONS

State Bar of Nita, Trust & Estates Section
Darrow County Bar Association, Trust & Estates Section
American Bar Association
National Academy of Elder Law Attorneys (NAELA)

TEACHING EXPERIENCE

Adjunct Professor of Estate Planning, St. Marks Nita Law College (Online), YR-4 to present.
Guest Lecturer, Nita State University, Course in Elder Law, YR-2

PRESENTATIONS

Darrow County Bar Association, Legal Standards Section – Clear and Present Danger of Legal Malpractice Lawsuits: What Law Schools Don't Teach You, YR-1

Nita City Chamber of Commerce Annual Convention - First, We Kill All the Lawyers, Revisited: Maybe We Limit That to Counsel For Plaintiffs, YR-3
State of Nita Retired Employees Association, Fourth Annual Forum – Benefits of the Use of Trusts v. Wills: Revocable v. Irrevocable Trusts, YR-4

PUBLICATIONS

Co-Author, Fannin, C. and Price, A., *Don't Bad Mouth the Irrevocable Trust,* Northern Nita Seniors Association Monthly Bulletin, June, YR-3.
Price, A., *The Rise of the American Trust*, Journal of Nita Estate Planners Association, May, YR-4

COMMITTEE APPOINTMENTS

Nita State Bar Association, Executive Department Liaison Committee, YR-2 to Present. Multidisciplinary team charged with analyzing administrative regulations and legislation and making recommendations to the Office of the Governor of The State of Nita.
Nita State Bar Association, Professional Responsibility Committee, YR-4 to YR-2. Responsibility for reviewing Nita State Bar disciplinary hearings and making recommendations for improvement in reporting, investigations and dispositions.

HONORS, AWARDS AND ACHIEVEMENTS

Outstanding Expert in Legal Malpractice, Northern Nita Civil Defense Counsel Association, October, YR-1

Exhibit 16

CURRICULUM VITAE PAT HARDESTY

PAT HARDESTY

BAKER & WILSON
1865 Professional Drive, Suite 101
Nita City, Nita 85523-2102
(555) 645-1101

Education

- YR-28 BA, Yale University
- YR-25 JD, University of California, Boalt Hall

Professional Experience

- Law Clerk, Ninth Circuit Court of Appeals, Hon. Geoffrey Allister, YR-25-23
- Associate Attorney, McAdams, Sullivan & Prescott, San Francisco, CA YR-23-20
- Associate Attorney, Baker, Wilson & Patterson, Nita City, Nita, YR-20-15
- Partner, Baker & Wilson, Nita City, Nita, YR-15 to present

Teaching Experience

- Nita University School of Law, Adjunct Professor in Estate Planning, Trusts, and Wills, YR-8 to present
- Nita State Bar Association Continuing Legal Education (CEB) Instructor in Estate Planning, Trusts, and Wills, YR-9 to present

Professional Certifications and Associations

- Certified Specialist, Estate Planning, Nita State Bar Association, YR-12 to present
- American Bar Association, Certification in Estate Planning, Wills, and Trusts, YR-10 to present
- Fellow, American College of Trust & Estate Counsel, YR-8 to present
- Chair, Nita Estate Planning and Probate Law Advisory Commission, YR-6-4

Awards

- Distinguished Member Award, Darrow County Association of Probate Counsel YR-4

Professional Publications

- Wrote chapter on Living Trusts in Thompson's text on Nita Trust Law, YR-7
- Essay entitled *"What is Professional Responsibility? Why should we worry about that?"*
- Assembled and edited extensive materials for CEB classes on Ethical and Malpractice Considerations in Estate Planning
- Article entitled *"Proving The Death of the Decedent Without A Body"* in the YR-7 CEB Estate Planning Newsletter
- Authored *"Don't Forget the Basics"* column three times for the Nita State Bar's Estate Planning Trust & Probate Law Section newsletter
- Authored article *"Changing Nature of the Family; the Future of Estate Planning"* for the September, YR-3 Nita State Bar Journal.

Expert Testimony

- In my work as a specialist in the fields of Estate Planning, Wills, and Trusts I have testified in both state and federal courts of law and been found to be a qualified expert in those fields in approximately twelve cases, eight of which have been for plaintiffs and four of which have been for defendants.

EXHIBIT 17

CIUDAD DE MANCORA DEPARTAMENTO DE POLICIA
Av. Piura 97
Ciudad de Mancora, Peru
Botica BTL Tele: 576221

REPORTE DE PERSONAS DESPARECIDAS
(THE FOLLOWING IS AN ENGLISH TRANSLATION)

FILE NUMBER:	PD - YR-2-14
MISSING PERSON:	April S. Huntington, aka April S. Zoldak
DESCRIPTION:	Female, 5'7, 125 pounds, DOB 01-14-YR-36, USA Social Security Number 644-29-5585
RESIDENCE:	1848 Lake Drive, # 210, Greenville, Nita, USA
OCCUPATION:	Investor
LAST CONTACT DATE:	March 6, YR-2
MENTAL/PHYSICAL CONDITION:	Unknown
DATE OF REPORT:	March 6, YR-2
REPORTED BY:	Mark Aster

BY COMMUNITY SERVICES OFFICER LUISA YBARRA, # 72

On March 6, YR-2 at 1315 hours I was contacted at the front desk by Mark Aster, an American, who seemed to be severely agitated. He stated that he had accompanied April Huntington to La Costa Magnifica and they had engaged in business dealings with representatives of both the resort and with the Peruvian Government, and after concluding those transactions, they went scuba diving. He said that somehow Huntington disappeared. Aster said that he panicked and looked for her, and when he could not find her in the ocean area where she was, he sought the aid of lifeguards. They too searched unsuccessfully, and later he discovered that all her belongings were gone. There was no sign of foul play such as a kidnapping. He said he was stunned, and he desperately needed help from police to find her.

I then contacted Detective Geraldo Villegas who Chief Diego assigned to conduct a follow-up investigation, and Detective Villegas proceeded to interview Aster to obtain more information.

I. By Detective Geraldo Villegas, # 23

On March 6, YR-2 at 1345 hours I was informed by Chief Diego that CSO Ybarra had spoken with an American man who claimed that the woman that he had accompanied to La Costa Magnifica had either drowned, had been kidnapped, or suddenly left La Costa without informing him. Chief Diego assigned me to follow-up the investigation as I was able to speak English. CSO Ybarra contacted me and introduced me to Mark Aster. Mr. Aster appeared highly agitated and said he was afraid that the woman, April Huntington, had drowned or been kidnapped. He told me that they had been scuba diving about ten kilometers north of La Costa Magnifica and she was suddenly gone. He said he searched the entire area and could not find a trace of her, so he surfaced and sought aid from lifeguards. He then thought perhaps for some reason she left and returned to the resort, so he went to the hotel and was advised that no one had seen her. He then immediately went to their room and found that she was gone and all of her belongings were gone. He then panicked and contacted the American Embassy, and he was advised to contact our department.

Aster claimed that April came to complete negotiations on a business transaction that involved the purchase of shares in the La Costa Magnifica resort and shares in the massive Peruvian Land and Mining development. He said the purchase amounted to about three quarters of a million American dollars. He expressed concern that someone could have known about this and kidnapped her for ransom. I then asked for more specifics about this alleged business agreement including the names of all the parties representing both the resort and the Peruvian Land and Mining Company. I then transported Aster to the hotel and spoke with several people including two desk clerks, the security officer, and two maids. Each informed me that they had not seen Huntington return at any time that morning. Each also indicated that there were many reasons why they might not have seen her even if she did return. They showed me the back entrance which was near a parking area.

Aster and I went with the security officer to Room 206, the room where Aster and Huntington were registered, and Aster described two suitcases, women's clothing that had been in the closet, and articles in the bathroom. I was unable to locate any articles that appeared to be the kind a woman would own. I was unable to find any note or message left by Huntington. I then asked Aster to provide copies of the investment agreement forms. He said that he did not have any. Since he was an attorney, I found that odd. I asked him if he came as a personal friend of Huntington, or whether he came because of his legal role. He said as a personal friend. There was only one set of forms, and apparently Huntington had those. He said that in an American trust the person who had the authority and responsibility for such negotiations was the trustee, and that was April Huntington. I was suspicious about his account, and informed Aster that he would not be allowed to return to the United States until we conducted further investigation. He seemed upset to hear this, but he said he would continue to stay at La Costa Magnifica until I authorized him to leave. I told him that by the end of the week we should have a firm answer as to when he could leave. I told Aster we would need to acquire more information about the investments by contacting representatives of the resort and the Land and Mining Company. He said that he would make every effort to check on this and report back to me.

After I left Aster, I returned to the front desk with Security Officer Armando Ruiz who said that in his mind there were some similarities to the famous case of Joran van der Sloot who killed the young woman in Aruba and the Peruvian woman. I admonished Ruiz not to make any verbal accusations like that before our department had the opportunity to check out Aster's story.

Next I contacted Joaquin Vera, the manager of La Costa Magnifica, and asked if Vera knew which lifeguards were on duty in the area where Aster and Huntington were scuba diving. Vera said that this was an area that had no government lifeguards, and as a resort accommodation for visitors who rent scuba diving equipment from La Costa Magnifica, the resort hires two lifeguards to handle any area where their residents dive. On April 6th there were two lifeguards on duty, and he referred me to one who was presently down in the rental shop. The lifeguard was an American who had lifeguard experience in the United States, and he was training Peruvians in the skill. He then walked me to the rental shop, and I spoke with the American, Spencer Wilson.

Wilson told me that he and Enrique Guzman, the other lifeguard, were covering the area of the beach near where Aster and Huntington were diving. Wilson received a cell call that there was an emergency three miles down the coast. They went there and found no emergency. Someone was swimming in an area marked unsafe, and they made the swimmer leave. About an hour after he got the call they returned and continued to monitor an area of about three or four miles. Aster was running down the beach yelling, and when he explained what happened to Huntington, both Wilson and Guzman grabbed scuba gear and searched the area of the caves and their surroundings, and found no sign of Huntington. Aster was frantic, and they took him back to the hotel. They never saw Huntington leave the beach, but they were not watching that area for at least one hour. If she had gotten out of the beach and brought her gear to a car and left, they would not have seen her. The gear was never returned to the shop, and employees of the hotel searched to try and find any such evidence around the hotel, and none was found. Wilson said that he suspected he would be in trouble with the management of the hotel, but it was a lifeguard's duty to respond to an emergency call of the kind he received.

I then contacted Vera again and asked who Daniela Medina was. Vera said he had never heard of her. This is the one who Aster said represented the resort in the negotiations. Vera said that it would be impossible for such negotiations to be conducted by someone without Vera knowing about the matter. Later at 1615 hours I phoned the offices of The Peruvian Land and Mining Company in Lima, and I spoke with their chief finance officer, Alfonso Garcia, who said that there was no person by the name of Gustavo Vega working for them or representing them in any financial dealings.

I then contacted headquarters in Lima and spoke with Lt. Emanuel Ruiz. I explained the facts and asked whether there were any reports of kidnappings or attempts to kidnap American citizens. He informed me that there had been two in the area of Cusco and they had information that kidnappers were planning on expanding their efforts in the tourist area of Machu Picchu. So far headquarters had no information identifying any suspects, but because of the serious consequences that could result from such crimes, headquarters had assigned three investigators to the two crimes. Lt. Ruiz said that there were no known kidnapping attempts or crimes of this kind outside of those two areas, but our office could certainly not rule out such crimes in other tourist areas of Peru. I informed him that our office found no signs of any such activity and our canvas of the beach and the hotel produced no evidence that April Huntington was kidnapped. Lt. Ruiz assured me that if his office developed any more evidence tending to prove that there was such a kidnapping or plans to kidnap Americans in the Mancora area, he would notify me immediately. I then obtained a copy of April Huntington's driver's license photo from the state of Nita Department of Motor Vehicles and circulated that throughout the Policia Nacional Del Peru offices. That photo is set out below.

On March 7, YR-2 at 0930 hours I received a call from Aster. He said that he had contacted officials in La Costa Magnifica and the Land and Mining Company and was informed by both that no one with the names he gave me was employed in their organizations. After discussing the matter with Chief Diego, we agreed that we had no legal cause to further detain Aster in Peru, and told him he had clearance to return to the United States. I informed him that I had checked with headquarters, and there was no evidence of any kidnappings in our area, and that if any such evidence developed, I would inform him. I also told him that if we received any information that further implicated him in Huntington's disappearance, we had assurance from both the Peru Attorney General's Office and the American Embassy that he could be extradited to Peru. Aster said that he understood and he appreciated my efforts to help solve this mystery, and that if he received any further information he would forward it to our office.

On March 13, YR-2 at 1315 hours Lt. Ruiz called and advised me that investigators in his office had spoken with confidential informants that they had used in identifying potential suspects in the Cusco kidnappings, and they were unaware of any kidnappings or plans to kidnap Americans in the Mancora area. He stated again that our office would immediately be alerted if they were to discover any such information.

Exhibit 18

PHOTO OF APRIL HUNTINGTON

ARREST AND CONVICTION RECORD OF APRIL HUNTINGTON

RE: SCHULTZ, HON. H. DCDC DATE: 12-20-YR-1 TIME: 1630
CIR/D8373522
SEX/F
DOB: 01-14-YR-36
NAM/01 HUNTINGTON, APRIL S.
NAM/02 ZOLDAK, APRIL S.
NDL/M9588312, STATUS VALID
SOC/644295585

****

#1

05-13-YR-4 CIT. NDA CC 476a-NON-SUFFICIENT FUNDS CHECKS, MISDEMEANOR
07-04-YR-4 PLEA OF NO CONTEST, CONVICTED C.C. 476a, MISDEMEANOR: SEN. 1 YEARS INFORMAL PROBATION, 40 HOURS SHERIFF'S WORK PROGRAM, RESTITUTION $4,285.00

****

#2

03-14-YR-3 ARREST. DCSO C.C. 484-GRAND THEFT, EMBEZZLEMENT, FELONY
06-02-YR-3 PLED GUILTY TO FELONY GRAND THEFT, 60 DAYS COUNTY JAIL, TWO YEARS FORMAL PROBATION, $8,540.00 RESTITUTION

<u>NOT TO BE DUPLICATED</u>

ARREST AND CONVICTION RECORD OF HAROLD J. ZOLDAK

RE: SCHULTZ, HON. H. DCDC DATE: 12-28-YR-2 TIME: 1630
CIR/D7693466
DOB: 01-14-YR-42
SEX: M
NAM/01 ZOLDAK, HAROLD J.
NAM/02 ZOLDAK, HARRY
NDL/D5477929
SOC/431078125

ARR/DET/CITE/CONV:
#1

07-03-YR-11 CIT. NAG NVC 28051-ALTER INDICATED VEHICLE MILEAGE, MISDEMEANOR
07-29-YR-11 CONVICTION, MISDEMEANOR NVC 28051, MISDEMEANOR, 2 YEARS PROBATION, RESTITUTION, FINE $5,500

****

#2

04-24-YR-7 ARREST NHP C.C. 23102a-DRIVING UNDER THE INFLUENCE OF ALCOHOL, MISDEMEANOR
05-27-YR-7 PLEA OF GUILTY C.C. 23102a,MISDEMEANOR, 3 YEARS INFORMAL PROBATION, 2 DAYS COUNTY JAIL.
09-12-YR-6 PROBATION VIOLATION
11-16-YR-6 PROBATION REVOKED, SENTENCE 60 DAYS COUNTY JAIL, CONSECUTIVE TO SENTENCE IN CASE #2

****

#3

07-04-YR-6 ARREST DPD C.C. 415-DISTURBING THE PEACE, MISDEMEANOR, C.C.148-RESISTING ARREST, AND C.C.647a-DRUNK IN PUBLIC
07-13-YR-6 PLEA OF GUILTY TO C.C. 647a-DRUNK IN PUBLIC, MISDEMEANOR AND C.C.148-RESISTING ARREST,MISDEMEANOR, 3 YEARS INFORMAL PROBATION, 3 MONTHS COUNTY JAIL, CONSECUTIVE TO CASE #1.FINE $940.

<u>NOT TO BE DUPLICATED</u>

Applicable Statutory Law

NITA State Probate Code

§ 317 Presumption of Revocability

(a) Unless a trust is expressly made irrevocable by the trust instrument, the trust is revocable by the settlor. Even where there is no doubt of the settlor's intent that the trust should be irrevocable, there is a presumption of revocability.

(b) "Expressly," for purposes of this statutory rule, means distinctly, clearly, unmistakably, or in direct terms, as distinguished from impliedly or inferentially.

(c) A settlor's conduct will not alter the nature of an irrevocable trust after it has been established.

§ 362 Trustee's Bond

(a) A trustee is not required to give a bond to secure performance of the trustee's duties, unless any of the following circumstances occurs:

A bond is required by the trust instrument.

Notwithstanding a waiver of a bond in the trust instrument, a bond is found by the court to be necessary to protect the interest of beneficiaries or other persons having an interest in the trust.

An individual who is not named as a trustee in the trust instrument is appointed as a trustee by the court.

(b) If a bond is required, it shall be filed or served and shall be in the amount and with sureties and liabilities ordered by the court.

(c) Except as otherwise provided in the trust instrument or ordered by the court, the cost of the bond shall be charged against the trust.

(d) A trust company may not be required to give a bond, notwithstanding a contrary provision in the trust instrument.

§ 364 Removal of Trustee; Grounds; Surrender of Property or Suspension of Powers

(a) A trustee may be removed in accordance with the trust instrument, by the court on its own motion, or on petition of a settlor, cotrustee, or beneficiary

(b) The grounds for removal of a trustee by the court including the following:

1) Where the trustee has committed a breach of the trust.

2) Where the trustee is insolvent or otherwise unfit to administer the trust.

3) Where hostility or lack of cooperation among cotrustees impairs the administration of the trust.

4) Where the trustee fails or declines to act.

5) Where the trustee's compensation is excessive under the circumstances.

6) For other good cause.

(c) If it appears to the court that trust property or the interest of a beneficiary may suffer loss or injury pending a decision on a petition for removal of a trustee and any appellate review, the court may, on its own or on petition of a cotrustee or beneficiary, compel the trustee whose removal is sought to surrender trust property to a cotrustee or to a receiver or temporary trustee. The court may also suspend the powers of the trustee to the extent the court deems necessary.

§ 402 Trustee's Duty of Loyalty

(a) The trustee has a duty to administer the trust solely in the interest of the beneficiaries.

§ 404 Conflicts of Interest

(a) The trustee has a duty not to use or deal with trust property for the trustee's own profit or for any other purpose unconnected with the trust, nor to take part in any transaction in which the trustee has an interest adverse to the beneficiary.

§ 414 Trustee's Standard of Care

(a) A trustee shall invest and manage trust assets as a prudent investor would, by considering the purposes, terms, distribution requirements, and other circumstances of the trust. In satisfying this standard, the trustee shall exercise reasonable care, skill, and caution.

(b) A trustee's investment and management decisions respecting individual assets and course of action must be evaluated not in isolation, but in the context of the trust portfolio as a whole and as part of an overall investment strategy having risk and return objectives reasonably suited to the trust.

(c) A trustee shall make a reasonable effort to ascertain facts relevant to the investment and management of trust assets.

(d) Compliance with the prudent investor rule is determined in light of the facts and circumstances existing at the time of a trustee's decision or action and not by hindsight.

§ 458 Trust Protector

(a) A trust instrument may provide for the appointment of a disinterested third party to act as a trust protector.

(b) A trust protector appointed under (a) of this section has the powers, delegations, and functions conferred on a protector by the trust instrument, which may include the power to:

1) remove and appoint a trustee;

2) approve trustee accounts;

3) advise the trust regarding beneficiaries;

4) interpret the terms of the trust; and

5) consent to, direct, or veto income or principal distribution.

(c) A trust protector is presumptively a fiduciary that, as such, is required to act in good faith with regard to the purposes of the trust and the interest of the beneficiaries. The holder of a power to direct is liable for any loss that results from breach of a fiduciary duty.

1) A settlor could provide in a trust instrument that the trust protector is not to be held to the standards of a fiduciary

(d) A trustee may refuse the direction of a trust protector only if the attempted exercise would be manifestly contrary to the terms of the trust or the trustee knows the attempted exercise would constitute a serious breach of a fiduciary duty owed by the trust protector to the beneficiaries of the trust.

§ 466 Standing and Set Aside of Irrevocable Trust

(a) In any lawsuit wherein there is an allegation that an irrevocable trust was executed based upon negligence, breach of fiduciary duty, undue influence, conversion, conspiracy, or other basis upon which the trust may possibly be set aside, the trustor of the irrevocable trust has standing to bring all causes of action notwithstanding the fact that the trust assets are technically in the name of the trust.

(b) The trustor may also ask the court for a finding and judgment that the irrevocable trust is set aside as part of the pending lawsuit.

NITA State Criminal Code

Nita Criminal Code §148 – Resisting, Delaying or Obstructing an Officer

1. Every person who willfully resists, delays, or obstructs any peace officer in the discharge or attempt to discharge any duty of his or her office or employment is guilty of a violation of this section.

2. A violation of this section shall be punished by a fine not exceeding one thousand dollars ($1,000), or by imprisonment in a county jail not to exceed one (1) year, or by both that fine and imprisonment.

Nita Vehicle Code §23152(a) – Driving Under the Influence

1. Any person who drives under the influence of any alcoholic beverage or drug is guilty of a misdemeanor.

2. Driving under the influence of alcohol or drugs is a misdemeanor punishable by confinement in the county jail for a period of not more than six (6) months and by a fine of not less than $400 nor more than one thousand dollars ($1000).

Nita Vehicle Code §28051 – Unlawful to Alter Indicated Mileage

1. Any person who disconnects, turns back, or resets the odometer of any motor vehicle with intent to alter the number of miles indicated on the odometer gauge is guilty of a misdemeanor.

2. A violation shall be punished by imprisonment in the county jail for a period of not more than six (6) months or by a fine of not more than five hundred dollars ($500), or by both such fine and imprisonment.

(c) A victor could provide, in [illegible] [illegible] [illegible] or [illegible] [illegible] the [illegible].

(d) [illegible]

[illegible]

(f) [illegible]

(g) The victor may attend the [illegible] [illegible] [illegible]

IV. In State Criminal Code

[illegible] Criminal Code [illegible] [illegible] in Office

[illegible]

[illegible]

[illegible]

[illegible]

[illegible]

[illegible]

[illegible]

EXCERPTS FROM

NITA RULES OF PROFESSIONAL CONDUCT

Scope

(20) Violation of a Rule should not itself give rise to a cause of action against a lawyer nor should it create any presumption in such a case that a legal duty has been breached. The Rules . . . are not designed to be a basis for civil liability. . . . Nevertheless, since the Rules do establish standards of conduct by lawyers, a lawyer's violation of a Rule may be evidence of breach of the applicable standard of conduct.

RULE 1.0 Terminology

. . . .

(e) "Informed consent" denotes the agreement by a person to a proposed course of conduct after the lawyer has communicated adequate information and explanation about the material risks of and reasonably available alternatives to the proposed course of conduct.

(f) "Knowingly," "known," or "knows" denotes actual knowledge of the fact in question. A person's knowledge may be inferred from circumstances.

(h) "Reasonable" or "reasonably" when used in relation to conduct by a lawyer denotes the conduct of a reasonably prudent and competent lawyer.

(i) "Reasonable belief" or "reasonably believes" when used in reference to a lawyer denotes that the lawyer believes the matter in question and that the circumstances are such that the belief is reasonable.

(j) "Reasonably should know" when used in reference to a lawyer denotes that a lawyer of reasonable prudence and competence would ascertain the matter in question.

. . . .

RULE 1.1 Competence

(a) A lawyer shall provide competent representation to a client. Competent representation requires the legal knowledge, skill, thoroughness, and preparation reasonably necessary for the representation.

Comment

Legal Knowledge and Skill

(1) In determining whether a lawyer employs the requisite knowledge and skill in a particular matter, relevant factors include the relative complexity and specialized nature of the matter, the lawyer's general experience, the lawyer's training and experience in the field in question, the preparation and study the lawyer is able to give the matter, and whether it is feasible to refer the matter to, or associate or consult with, a lawyer of established competence in the field in question. In many instances, the required proficiency is that of a general practitioner. Expertise in a particular field of law may be required in some circumstances.

(2) A lawyer need not necessarily have special training or prior experience to handle legal problems of a type with which the lawyer is unfamiliar. A newly admitted lawyer can be as competent as a practitioner with long experience. Some important legal skills, such as the analysis of precedent, the evaluation of evidence, and legal drafting, are required in all legal problems. Perhaps the most fundamental legal skill consists of determining what kind of legal problems a situation may involve, a skill that necessarily transcends any particular specialized knowledge. A lawyer can provide adequate representation in a wholly novel field through necessary study. Competent representation can also be provided through the association of a lawyer of established competence in the field in question.

(4) A lawyer may accept representation where the requisite level of competence can be achieved by reasonable preparation. . . .

Thoroughness and Preparation

(5) Competent handling of a particular matter includes inquiry into and analysis of the factual and legal elements of the problem, and use of methods and procedures meeting the standards of competent practitioners. It also includes adequate preparation. The required attention and preparation are determined in part by what is at stake; major litigation and complex transactions ordinarily require more extensive treatment than matters of lesser complexity and consequence. An agreement between the lawyer and the client regarding the scope of the representation may limit the matters for which the lawyer is responsible. See Rule 1.2(c).

Maintaining Competence

(1) To maintain the requisite knowledge and skill, a lawyer should keep abreast of changes in the law and its practice, engage in continuing study and education, and comply with all continuing legal education requirements to which the lawyer is subject.

RULE 1.2 Scope of Representation and Allocation of Authority Between Client and Lawyer

(a) A lawyer shall abide by a client's decisions concerning the objectives of representation and, as required by Rule 1.4, shall consult with the client as to the means by which they are to be pursued. A lawyer may take such action on behalf of the client as is impliedly authorized to carry out the representation. . . . In a criminal case, the lawyer shall abide by the client's decision, after consultation with the lawyer, . . . whether the client will testify.

Comment

Allocation of Authority between Client and Lawyer

(1) Paragraph (a) confers upon the client the ultimate authority to determine the purposes to be served by legal representation, within the limits imposed by law and the lawyer's professional obligations. The decisions specified in paragraph (a), such as whether to settle a civil matter, must also be made by the client. See Rule 1.4(a)(1) for the lawyer's duty to communicate with the client about such decisions. With respect to the means by which the client's objectives are to be pursued, the lawyer shall consult with the client as required by Rule 1.4(a)(2) and may take such action as is impliedly authorized to carry out the representation.

(2) On occasion, however, a lawyer and a client may disagree about the means to be used to accomplish the client's objectives. Clients normally defer to the special knowledge and skill of their lawyer

with respect to the means to be used to accomplish their objectives, particularly with respect to technical, legal and tactical matters. Conversely, lawyers usually defer to the client regarding such questions as the expense to be incurred and concern for third persons who might be adversely affected. Because of the varied nature of the matters about which a lawyer and client might disagree and because the actions in question may implicate the interests of a tribunal or other persons, this Rule does not prescribe how many disagreements are to be resolved. Other law, however, may be applicable and should be consulted by the lawyer. The lawyer should also consult with the client and seek a mutually acceptable resolution of the disagreement. If such efforts are unavailing and the lawyer has a fundamental disagreement with the client, the lawyer may withdraw from the representation. . . . Conversely, the client may resolve the disagreement by discharging the lawyer. . . .

RULE 1.4 Communication

(a) A lawyer shall:

(1) promptly inform the client of any decision or circumstance with respect to which the client's informed consent, as defined in Rule 1.0(e), is required by these Rules;

(2) reasonably consult with the client about the means by which the client's objectives are to be accomplished;

(3) keep the client reasonably informed about the status of the matter; [and]

(4) promptly comply with reasonable requests for information;. . .

(b) A lawyer shall explain a matter to the extent reasonably necessary to permit the client to make informed decisions regarding the representation.

Comment:

(1) Reasonable communication between the lawyer and the client is necessary for the client effectively to participate in the representation.

Communicating with Client

(2) If these Rules require that a particular decision about the representation be made by the client, paragraph (a)(1) requires that the lawyer promptly consult with and secure the client's consent prior to taking action unless prior discussions with the client have resolved what action the client wants the lawyer to take. . . .

(3) Paragraph (a)(2) requires the lawyer to reasonably consult with the client about the means to be used to accomplish the client's objectives. In some situations – depending on both the importance of the action under consideration and the feasibility of consulting with the client – this duty will require consultation prior to taking action. In other circumstances, such as during a trial when an immediate decision must be made, the exigency of the situation may require the lawyer to act without prior consultation. In such cases the lawyer must nonetheless act reasonably to inform the client of actions the lawyer has taken on the client's behalf. Additionally, paragraph (a)(3) requires that the lawyer keep the client reasonably informed about the status of the matter, such as significant developments affecting the timing or the substance of the representation.

(4) A lawyer's regular communication with clients will minimize the occasions on which a client will need to request information concerning the representation. When a client makes a reasonable request

for information, however, paragraph (a)(4) requires prompt compliance with the request, or if a prompt response is not feasible, that the lawyer, or a member of the lawyer's staff, acknowledge receipt of the request and advise the client when a response may be expected. Client telephone calls should be promptly returned or acknowledged.

Explaining Matters

(5) The client should have sufficient information to participate intelligently in decisions concerning the objectives of the representation and the means by which they are to be pursued, to the extent the client is willing and able to do so. Adequacy of communication depends in part on the kind of advice or assistance that is involved. . . . In litigation a lawyer should explain the general strategy and prospects of success and ordinarily should consult the client on tactics that are likely to result in significant expense . . . . On the other hand, a lawyer ordinarily will not be expected to describe trial or negotiation strategy in detail. The guiding principle is that the lawyer should fulfill reasonable client expectations for information consistent with the duty to act in the client's best interests, and the client's overall requirements as to the character of representation. In certain circumstances, such as when a lawyer asks a client to consent to a representation affected by a conflict of interest, the client must give informed consent, as defined in Rule 1.0(e);

(6) Ordinarily, the information to be provided is that appropriate for a client who is a comprehending and responsible adult. . . . Where many routine matters are involved, a system of limited or occasional reporting may be arranged with the client.

Withholding Information

(7) In some circumstances, a lawyer may be justified in delaying transmission of information when the client would be likely to react imprudently to an immediate communication. . . . A lawyer may not withhold information to serve the lawyer's own interest or convenience or the interests or convenience of another person. . . .

RULE 1.6 Confidentiality of Information

a) A lawyer shall not reveal information relating to the representation of a client unless the client gives informed consent [or] the disclosure is impliedly authorized in order to carry out the representation . . . .

Comment

(2) A fundamental principle in the client-lawyer relationship is that, in the absence of the client's informed consent, the lawyer must not reveal information relating to the representation. See Rule 1.0(e) for the definition of informed consent. This contributes to the trust that is the hallmark of the client-lawyer relationship. The client is thereby encouraged to seek legal assistance and to communicate fully and frankly with the lawyer even as to embarrassing or legally damaging subject matter. . . .

(3) . . . The rule of client-lawyer confidentiality applies in situations other than those where evidence is sought from the lawyer through compulsion of law. The confidentiality rule, for example, applies not only to matters communicated in confidence by the client but also to all information relating to the representation, whatever its source. A lawyer may not disclose such information except as authorized by law or required by the Rules of Professional Conduct or other law. . . .

RULE 1.8 Conflict of Interest; Current Clients; Specific Rules

(f) A lawyer shall not accept compensation for representing a client from one other than the client unless:

(1) the client gives informed consent;

(2) there is no interference with the lawyer's independence of professional judgment or with the client-lawyer relationship; and

(3) information relating to representation of a client is protected as required by Rule.

(j) A lawyer shall not have sexual relations with a client unless a consensual sexual relationship existed between them when the client-lawyer relationship commenced.

Comment

Person Paying for a Lawyer's Services

(11) Lawyers are frequently asked to represent a client under circumstances in which a third person will compensate the lawyer, in whole or in part. The third person might be a relative or friend, an indemnitor (such as a liability insurance company) or a co-client (such as a corporation sued along with one or more of its employees). Because third-party payers frequently have interests that differ from those of the client, including interests in minimizing the amount spent on the representation and in learning how the representation is progressing, lawyers are prohibited from accepting or continuing such representations unless the lawyer determines that there will be no interference with the lawyer's independent professional judgment and there is informed consent from the client. See also Rule 5.4(c) (prohibiting interference with a lawyer's professional judgment by one who recommends, employs or pays the lawyer to render legal services for another).

(12) Sometimes, it will be sufficient for the lawyer to obtain the client's informed consent regarding the fact of the payment and the identity of the third-party payer. If, however, the fee arrangement creates a conflict of interest for the lawyer, then the lawyer must comply with Rule 1.7. The lawyer must also conform to the requirements of Rule 1.6 concerning confidentiality. Under Rule 1.7(a), a conflict of interest exists if there is significant risk that the lawyer's representation of the client will be materially limited by the lawyer's own interest in the fee arrangement or by the lawyer's responsibilities to the third-party payer (for example, when the third-party payer is a co-client). Under Rule 1.7(b), the lawyer may accept or continue the representation with the informed consent of each affected client, unless the conflict is nonconsentable under that paragraph. Under Rule 1.7(b), the informed consent must be confirmed in writing.

Client-Lawyer Sexual Relationships

(17) The relationship between lawyer and client is a fiduciary one in which the lawyer occupies the highest position of trust and confidence. The relationship is almost always unequal; thus, a sexual relationship between lawyer and client can involve unfair exploitation of the lawyer's fiduciary role, in violation of the lawyer's basic ethical obligation not to use the trust of the client to the client's disadvantage. In addition, such a relationship presents a significant danger that, because of the lawyer's emotional involvement, the lawyer will be unable to represent the client without impairment of the exercise of independent professional judgment. Moreover, a blurred line between the professional and personal relationships may make it difficult to predict to what extent client confidences will be protected

by the attorney-client evidentiary privilege, since client confidences are protected by privilege only when they are imparted in the context of the client-lawyer relationship. Because of the significant danger of harm to client interests and because the client's own emotional involvement renders it unlikely that the client could give adequate informed consent, this Rule prohibits the lawyer from having sexual relations with a client regardless of whether the relationship is consensual and regardless of the absence of prejudice to the client.

(18) Sexual relationships that predate the client-lawyer relationship are not prohibited. Issues relating to the exploitation of the fiduciary relationship and client dependency are diminished when the sexual relationship existed prior to the commencement of the client-lawyer relationship. However, before proceeding with the representation in these circumstances, the lawyer should consider whether the lawyer's ability to represent the client will be materially limited by the relationship. See Rule 1.7(a)(2).

(19) When the client is an organization, paragraph (j) of this Rule prohibits a lawyer for the organization (whether inside counsel or outside counsel) from having a sexual relationship with a constituent of the organization who supervises, directs, or regularly consults with that lawyer concerning the organization's legal matters.

ANNOTATION

Rule 1.8 addresses ten specific situations in which a lawyer's own interests may compromise a client's representation or otherwise harm a client's interests. In most of these situations, the conflict cannot be cured by informed client consent. The lawyer must either avoid the situation entirely or comply with conditions designed to protect the client from overreaching by the lawyer.

2002 AMENDMENTS

Several subsections and corresponding comments were amended in 2002. Family relationships among lawyers, formerly the subject of subsection (i), are now addressed in Comment [11] to Rule 1.7. Former subsection (j) (acquiring a proprietary interest in litigation) was renumbered as subsection (i), and a new subsection (j) was added to prohibit most client-lawyer sexual relationships. Subsection (k) was added to impute to firm colleagues all but one (sex with clients) of Rule 1.8's prohibitions; until this amendment, none of the rule's prohibitions were to be imputed except gifts to lawyers. American Bar Association, *A Legislative History: The Development of the ABA Model Rules of Professional Conduct, 1982–2005*, at 210 (2006).

Subsection (f): Person Paying for Lawyer's Services

The most common situation in which a lawyer is paid by someone other than the client is insurance defense work, but the situation also arises when parents hire counsel for their children, when employers pay employees' legal expenses, and when friends or relatives pay for criminal defendants' counsel. Comment [11] observes that third-party payors frequently have interests separate from those of the client, including an interest in minimizing legal fees and an interest in finding out about the case's progress. For these reasons, Rule 1.8(f) imposes three conditions on acceptance of third-party payment: the client must give informed consent, there must be no interference with the lawyer's independence of professional judgment or with the client-lawyer relationship, and information relating to the representation must be protected as required by Rule 1.6. Directly related to this is Rule 5.4(c), which prohibits a lawyer from permitting the person paying for the lawyer's services to "direct or regulate the lawyer's professional judgment." *See, e.g.*, ABA Formal Ethics Op. 02-428 (2002) (lawyer may draft will for testator at request of existing client who pays lawyer and is potential beneficiary, provided testator gives informed consent and requirements of Rule 1.8(f) as well as Rule 5.4(c) satisfied). *See generally* Nancy J. Moore, *Ethical Issues in Third-Party Payment: Beyond the Insurance Defense Paradigm*, 16 Rev. Litig. 585 (Summer 1997).

Comment [12] also notes the applicability of Rule 1.7 in situations where the fee arrangement creates a conflict of interest for the lawyer. Although the two rules use different criteria—material limitation in Rule 1.7, and "interference with the lawyer's independence of professional judgment or with the client-lawyer relationship" in Rule 1.8(f)—no different substantive standard was apparently intended. *See* Geoffrey C. Hazard, Jr., W. William Hodes & Peter R. Jarvis, *The Law of Lawyering* § 12.13 (3d ed. 2001 & Supp. 2004).

Client-Lawyer Sexual Relationships

Rule 1.8(j) was added to the Model Rules in 2002, after several jurisdictions had adopted specific rules regarding client-lawyer sexual relations. "Although recognizing that most egregious behavior of lawyers can be addressed through other Rules[,] . . . having a specific Rule has the advantage not only of alerting lawyers more effectively to the dangers of sexual relationships with clients but also of alerting clients that the lawyer may have violated ethical obligations in engaging in such conduct." American Bar Association, *A Legislative History: The Development of the ABA Model Rules of Professional Conduct, 1982–2005*, at 209 (2006). Jurisdictions without specific rules had addressed client-lawyer sex under rules dealing with misconduct or conflicts of interest. *See, e.g., In re Rinella*, 677 N.E.2d 909 (Ill. 1997) (lawyer who had sexual relations with three matrimonial clients overreached and took advantage of his position; lack of explicit prohibition no defense); *In re Berg*, 955 P.2d 1240 (Kan. 1998) (sexual relations with vulnerable divorce clients violated several ethics rules and warranted disbarment despite lack of express prohibition); *see also* ABA Formal Ethics Op. 92-364 (1992) (fundamental principle of lawyer's fiduciary obligation to client, recognized in Rule 1.8, implies lawyer should not abuse client's trust by taking sexual or emotional advantage); *cf. In re Bash*, 880 N.E.2d 1182 (Ind. 2008) (attempted sexual relations with client violated Rule 8.4(a)).

Rule 1.8(j) prohibits all client-lawyer sexual relationships, including consensual relationships, except those predating the formation of the client-lawyer relationship. The per se prohibition recognizes the fiduciary nature of the client-lawyer relationship and the significant dangers of exploitation and impaired independence of professional judgment. *See In re Overboe*, 724 N.W.2d 576 (N.D. 2006) (pattern of inappropriate sexual conduct with clients); *State ex rel. Okla. Bar Ass'n v. Downes*, 121 P.3d 1058 (Okla. 2005) (multiple acts of misconduct, including consensual sex with client). Sexual relationships that predate the client-lawyer relationship are exempt from Rule 1.8(j) because concerns for exploitation and client dependency are thought to be diminished in such situations, but Comment [18] cautions that the lawyer must nevertheless consider whether the relationship will pose a material limitation on the representation within the meaning of Rule 1.7(a)(2).When the client is an organization, Comment [19] clarifies that the prohibition is limited to relationships with constituents of the organization who supervise, direct, or regularly consult with the lawyer about the organization's legal matters.

JURY INSTRUCTIONS

PART I. PRELIMINARY INSTRUCTIONS GIVEN PRIOR TO EVIDENCE

1.01 INTRODUCTION

You have been selected as jurors and have taken an oath to well and truly try this case. During the progress of the trial, there will be periods of time when the court recesses. During those periods, you must not talk to any of the parties, their lawyers, or any of the witnesses. If any attempt is made by anyone to talk to you concerning the matters here under consideration, you should immediately report the fact to the court.

You should keep an open mind. You should not form or express an opinion during the trial and should reach no conclusion in this case until you have hear all the evidence, the arguments of counsel, and the final instructions as to the law that will be given to you.

1.02 CONDUCT OF THE TRIAL

First, the attorneys will have the opportunity to make opening statements. These statements are not evidence and should only be considered as an outline of what the attorneys expect the evidence to show.

Next, the jury will hear the evidence. The plaintiff will present evidence first. When the plaintiff has finished, the defense will have an opportunity to present her evidence. Each witness will first be questioned by the side that asked the witness to testify. This is called direct examination. Then the other side is permitted to question the witness. This is called cross-examination.

Documents or objects referred to during the trial are called exhibits. Exhibits are given a number and marked so they may be clearly identified. Exhibits are not evidence until I admit them into evidence. During your deliberations, you will be able to look at all exhibits admitted into evidence.

There are many rules that govern whether something will be considered evidence in the trial. As one side presents evidence, the other side has the right to object and to ask me to decide if the evidence is permitted by the rules. Usually, I will decide immediately, but sometimes I may have to hear arguments outside of your presence.

After the evidence has been presented, I will instruct you on the law that applies to the case and the attorneys will make closing arguments. What the parties say in closing argument is not evidence. The arguments are offered to help you understand the evidence and how the law applies to it.

PART II. FINAL INSTRUCTIONS

1.00 RESPECTIVE DUTIES OF JUDGE AND JURY

Ladies and Gentlemen of the Jury:

You have heard all the evidence and the arguments of the attorneys, and it is now my duty to instruct you on the law.

The law applicable to this case is stated in these instructions, and it is your duty to follow all of them. You must not single out certain instructions and disregard others.

It is your duty to determine the facts, and to determine them *only* from the evidence in this case. You are to apply the law to the facts and in this way decide the case. You must not be governed or influenced by sympathy or prejudice for or against any party in this case. Your verdict must be based on evidence and not upon speculation, guess or conjecture.

From time to time the court has ruled on the admissibility of evidence. You must not concern yourselves with the reasons for these rulings. You should simply disregard questions and exhibits that were withdrawn due to a sustained objection.

The evidence that you should consider consists only of the witnesses' testimony and the exhibits. Any evidence that was received for a limited purpose should not be considered by you for any other purpose. You may consider all the evidence in light of your own observations and experiences in life.

Neither by these instructions, nor by any ruling or remark that I have made, do I indicate any opinion as to the facts or as to what the verdict should be.

2.00 EVIDENCE

Sworn testimony, documents, or anything else may be admitted into evidence. You must decide what the facts are in this case from the evidence you see or hear during the trial. You may not consider as evidence anything that you see or hear when court is not in session. What the attorneys say during the trial, including opening statements and closing arguments, is not evidence. Attorneys' questions are not evidence. Only the witnesses' answers are evidence. If the attorneys for both sides agree that certain facts are true, this agreement is called a stipulation. No other proof is needed and you must accept those facts as true in this trial.

Each side may object to evidence offered by the other side. If I overrule an objection, the witness will answer and you may consider the evidence. If I sustain an objection, you must ignore the question. If the witness did not answer, you must not guess what he or she might have said or why I sustained the objection. If the witness has already answered, you must ignore the answer. Also, if I grant a motion to strike testimony that you have heard, you must totally disregard that testimony and treat it as though it did not exist.

2.01 DIRECT AND INDIRECT EVIDENCE

Evidence can come in many forms. It can be testimony about what someone saw, heard, or smelled. It can be an exhibit admitted into evidence. It can be someone's opinion. Some evidence proves a fact directly, such as testimony of a witness who saw a jet plane flying across the sky. Some evidence proves a fact indirectly, such as testimony of a witness who saw only the white trail that jet planes often leave. This indirect evidence is referred to as "circumstantial evidence." In either instance, the witness's testimony is evidence that a jet plane flew across the sky. As far as the law is concerned, it makes no difference whether evidence is direct or indirect. You may choose to believe or disbelieve either kind. Whether it is direct or indirect, you should give every piece of evidence whatever weight you think it deserves.

2.02 WILLFUL SUPPRESSION OF EVIDENCE

You may consider whether one party intentionally concealed or destroyed evidence. If you decide that a party did so, you may decide that the evidence would have been unfavorable to that party.

2.03 DEPOSITION AS SUBSTANTIVE EVIDENCE

During the trial, you heard testimony read from a deposition. A deposition is the testimony of a person taken before trial. At a deposition the person is sworn to tell the truth and is questioned by the attorneys. You must consider the deposition testimony that was read to you the same way as you consider testimony given in court.

2.04 WITNESSES

A witness is a person who has knowledge related to this case. You will have to decide whether you believe each witness and how important each witness's testimony is to the case. You may believe all, part, or none of a witness's testimony. In deciding whether to believe a witness's testimony, you may consider among other factors the following:

- How well did the witness see, hear, or otherwise sense what he or she described in court?
- How well did the witness remember and describe what happened?
- How did the witness look, act, and speak while testifying?
- Did the witness have any reason to say something that was not true? Did the witness show any bias or prejudice? Did the witness have a personal relationship with any of the parties in the case? Does the witness have a personal stake in how this case is decided?
- What was the witness's attitude toward this case or about giving testimony?

Sometimes a witness may say something that is not consistent with something else he or she said. Sometimes different witnesses will give different versions of what happened. People often forget things or make mistakes in what they remember. Also, two people may see the same event but remember it differently. You may consider these differences, but do not decide that testimony is untrue just because it differs from other testimony.

However, if you decide that a witness deliberately testified untruthfully about something important, you may choose not to believe anything that witness said. But, if you think the witness testified untruthfully about some things but told the truth about others, you may accept the part you think is true and ignore the rest. Do not make any decision simply because there were more witnesses on one side than the other. If you believe it is true, the testimony of a single witness is enough to prove a fact. You must not be biased in favor of or against any witness because of his or her disability, gender, race, religion, ethnicity, sexual orientation, age, national origin, or socioeconomic status.

2.05 PRIOR CONVICTION OF A CRIMINAL OFFENSE

You have heard that a witness in this trial has been convicted of a criminal offense. You were told about the conviction only to help you decide whether you should believe the witness. You must not consider it for any other purpose.

2.06 STATEMENTS OF A PARTY OPPONENT

A party may offer into evidence any oral or written statement made by an opposing party outside the courtroom. When you evaluate such evidence you should consider whether you believe that the party actually made the statement. If you do not believe that, you may not consider the statement. If you do believe the statement was made, you should consider whether it was reported accurately. You should view testimony about an oral statement made by a party outside the courtroom with caution.

2.07 EXPERT WITNESS TESTIMONY

During the trial you heard testimony from expert witnesses. The law allows an expert to state opinions about matters in his or her field of expertise even if he or she has not witnessed any of the events involved in the trial. You do not have to accept an expert's opinion. As with any other witness, it is up to you to decide whether you believe the expert testimony and choose to use it as a basis for your decision. You may believe all, part, or none of an expert's testimony. In deciding whether to believe such testimony, you should consider the expert's training and experience, the facts the expert relied on, and the reasons for the expert's opinion.

If the expert witnesses disagreed with one another, you should weigh each opinion against the others. You should examine the reasons given for each opinion and the facts or other matter that each witness relied on. You may also compare the experts' qualifications.

2.08 OPINION TESTIMONY OF LAY WITNESS

A witness who was not an expert gave an opinion during the trial. You may, but are not required to, accept that opinion. You may give the opinion whatever weight you think is appropriate. Consider the extent of the witness's opportunity to perceive the matters on which the opinion is based, the reasons the witness gave for the opinion, and the facts or information on which the witness relied in forming that opinion. You must decide whether information on which the witness relied was true and accurate. You may disregard all or any part of an opinion that you find unbelievable, unreasonable, or unsupported by the evidence.

3.00 OBLIGATION TO PROVE

A party must persuade you, by the evidence presented in court, that what he or she is required to prove is more likely to be true than not true. This is referred to as "the burden of proof." After weighing all of the evidence, if you cannot decide that something is more likely to be true than not true, you must conclude that the party did not prove it. You should consider all the evidence, no matter which party produced the evidence.

In criminal trials, the prosecution must prove that the defendant is guilty beyond a reasonable doubt. But in civil trials, such as this one, the party who is required to prove something need prove only that it is more likely to be true than not true.

Certain facts must be proved by clear and convincing evidence, which is a higher burden of proof. This means the party must persuade you that it is highly probable that the fact is true. I will tell you specifically which facts must be proved by clear and convincing evidence.

4.00 PROFESSIONAL NEGLIGENCE – STANDARD OF CARE

A lawyer is negligent if he fails to use the skill and care that a reasonably careful lawyer would have used in similar circumstances. This level of skill, knowledge, and care is sometimes referred to as "the standard of care."

You must determine the level of skill and care that a reasonably careful lawyer would use in similar circumstances based only on the testimony of the expert witnesses, including Mark Aster, who have testified in this case.

4.01 DAMAGES FOR NEGLIGENT HANDLING OF LEGAL MATTER

To recover damages from Mark Aster, Rose Huntington must prove that she would have obtained a better result if Mark Aster had acted as a reasonably careful attorney.

5.00 FIDUCIARY DUTY EXPLAINED

A lawyer owes what is known as a fiduciary duty to his client. A fiduciary duty imposes on a lawyer a duty to act with the utmost good faith in the best interests of his client.

5.01 BREACH OF FIDUCIARY DUTY BY ATTORNEY – ESSENTIAL FACTUAL ELEMENTS

Rose Huntington claims that she was harmed because Mark Aster breached an attorney's duty owed to a client. To establish this claim, Rose Huntington must prove all of the following:

1. That Mark Aster was Rose Huntington's lawyer;
2. That Rose Huntington was harmed; and
3. That Mark Aster's conduct was a substantial factor in causing Rose Huntington's harm.

5.02 FAILURE TO USE REASONABLE CARE – ESSENTIAL FACTUAL ELEMENTS

Rose Huntington claims that she was harmed by Mark Aster's breach of the fiduciary duty to use reasonable care. To establish this claim, Rose Huntington must prove all of the following:

1. That Mark Aster was Rose Huntington's lawyer;
2. That Mark Aster acted on Rose Huntington's behalf for purposes of the trust instrument;
3. That Mark Aster failed to act as a reasonably careful lawyer would have acted under the same or similar circumstances;
4. That Rose Huntington was harmed; and
5. That Mark Aster's conduct was a substantial factor in causing Rose Huntington's harm.

5.03 DUTY OF UNDIVIDED LOYALTY – ESSENTIAL FACTUAL ELEMENTS

Rose Huntington claims that she was harmed by Mark Aster's breach of the fiduciary duty of undivided loyalty. A lawyer owes his client undivided loyalty. To establish this claim, Rose Huntington must prove all of the following:

1. That Mark Aster was Rose Huntington's lawyer;
2. That Mark Aster knowingly acted against Rose Huntington's interests in connection with her estate planning;

3. That Rose Huntington did not give informed consent to Mark Aster's conduct;
4. That Rose Huntington was harmed; and
5. That Mark Aster's conduct was a substantial factor in causing Rose Huntington's harm.

5.04 DUTY OF CONFIDENTIALITY – ESSENTIAL FACTUAL ELEMENTS

Rose Huntington claims that she was harmed by Mark Aster's breach of the fiduciary duty of confidentiality. To establish this claim, Rose Huntington must prove all of the following:

1. That Mark Aster was Rose Huntington's lawyer;
2. That Mark Aster had information relating to Rose Huntington that he knew or should have known was confidential;
3. That Mark Aster either
4. used Rose Huntington's confidential information for his own benefit; or
5. communicated Rose Huntington's confidential information to third parties;
6. That Rose Huntington did not give informed consent to Mark Aster's conduct;
7. That the confidential information was not a matter of general knowledge;
8. That Rose Huntington was harmed; and
9. That Mark Aster's conduct was a substantial factor in causing Rose Huntington's harm.

6.00 CONVERSION – ESSENTIAL FACTUAL ELEMENTS

Rose Huntington claims that Mark Aster wrongfully exercised control over her personal property. To establish this claim, Rose Huntington must prove all of the following:

1. That Rose Huntington owned personal assets;
2. That Mark Aster intentionally and substantially interfered with Rose Huntington's property by:

    taking possession of the assets;

    preventing Rose Huntington from having access to the assets;

    destroying the assets; or

    refusing to return the assets after Rose Huntington demanded their return.

7.00 AIDING AND ABETTING TORT – ESSENTIAL FACTUAL ELEMENTS

Rose Huntington claims that she was harmed by April Huntington's conversion and that Mark Aster is responsible for the harm because he aided and abetted April Huntington in committing the conversion.

If you find that April Huntington committed a conversion that harmed Rose Huntington, then you must determine whether Mark Aster is also responsible for the harm. Mark Aster is responsible as an aider and abetter if Rose Huntington proves all of the following:

1. That Mark Aster knew that a conversion was being committed by April Huntington against Rose Huntington;
2. That Mark Aster gave substantial assistance or encouragement April Huntington; and
3. That Mark Aster's conduct was a substantial factor in causing harm to Rose Huntington.

Mere knowledge that a conversion was being committed and the failure to prevent it do not constitute aiding and abetting.

8.00 DAMAGES – INTRODUCTION TO TORT DAMAGES – LIABILITY CONTESTED

If you decide that Rose Huntington has proved her claim against Mark Aster, you also must decide how much money will reasonably compensate to Rose Huntington for the harm. This compensation is called "damages." The amount of damages must include an award for each item of harm that was caused by Mark Aster's wrongful conduct, even if the particular harm could not have been anticipated.

Rose Huntington does not have to prove the exact amount of damages that will provide reasonable compensation for the harm. However, you must not speculate or guess in awarding damages.

The following are the specific items of damages claimed by Rose Huntington:

1. Damage to Personal Property
2. Loss or Destruction of Personal Property

The damages in this case are limited to the sum of $750,000. Any other damage issues are bifurcated by the court for a court determination at a later proceeding.

8.01 DAMAGE TO PERSONAL PROPERTY (ECONOMIC DAMAGE)

1. The harm to Rose Huntington's Ace Investment account.

To recover damages for harm to personal property, Rose Huntington must prove the reduction in the Ace Investment account's value or the reasonable cost of repairing it, whichever is less. [If there is evidence of both, Rose Huntington is entitled to the lesser of the two amounts.]

To determine the reduction in value, you must determine the fair market value of the Ace Investment account before the harm occurred and then subtract the fair market value of the Ace Investment account immediately after the harm occurred.

"Fair market value" is the highest price that a willing buyer would have paid to a willing seller, assuming:

1. That there is no pressure on either one to buy or sell; and
2. That the buyer and seller are fully informed of the condition and quality of the Ace Investment account.

8.02 LOSS OR DESTRUCTION OF PERSONAL PROPERTY (ECONOMIC DAMAGES)

2. The loss of Rose Huntington's investment capital in her Ace Investment account.

To recover damages for the loss Rose Huntington must prove the fair market value of the Ace Investment account just before the harm occurred.

"Fair market value" is the highest price that a willing buyer would have paid to a willing seller, assuming:

1. That there is no pressure on either one to buy or sell; and
2. That the buyer and seller are fully informed of the condition and quality of the Ace Investment account.

9.00 DECLARATION OF SET-ASIDE TRUST

During the trial the parties may have referred to the plaintiff's request to have the Trust "set aside." This remedy is not one you need to concern yourselves with in your deliberations. Based on your findings on Counts I-III, the court will determine whether this remedy should be granted.

10.00 APPLICABILITY OF NITA STATE BAR RULES OF PROFESSIONAL CONDUCT

Proof of a violation of a rule regulating the conduct of lawyers (*e.g.*, the Nita State Bar Rules of Professional Conduct) does not by itself give rise to an implied cause of action for professional negligence. However, such a violation may be considered by you as the trier of fact as an aid in understanding and applying the standard of negligence set forth in Instructions 4.00 and 5.01, to the extent that: (a) the rule was designed for the protection of persons in the position of the Plaintiff, and (b) proof of the content and construction of such a rule is relevant to the Plaintiff's claims.

11.00 CONCLUDING INSTRUCTIONS

The court did not in any way, and does not by these instructions, give or intimate any opinions as to what has or has not been proven in this case, or as to what are or are not the facts. You must not be concerned with the wisdom of any rule of law. It would be a violation of your sworn duty to base a verdict upon any other view of the law than that given by this court.

When you go to the jury room, the first thing you should do is choose a presiding juror. The presiding juror should see to it that your discussions are orderly and that everyone has a fair chance to be heard. It is your duty to talk with one another in the jury room and to consider the views of all the jurors. Each of you must decide the case for yourself, but only after you have considered the evidence with the other members of the jury. Feel free to change your mind if you are convinced that your position should be different. You should all try to agree, but do not give up your honest beliefs just because the others think differently.

Please do not state your opinions too strongly at the beginning of your deliberations. Also, do not immediately announce how you plan to vote. Keep an open mind so that you and your fellow jurors can easily share ideas about the case. You should use your common sense, but do not use or consider special training or unique personal experiences that any of you have in matters involved in this case. Your training or experience is not part of the evidence received in this case.

At least three quarters of the jurors must agree on each verdict and on each question that you are asked to answer. However, the same jurors do not have to agree on each verdict or each question. As soon as you have agreed on a verdict and answered all the questions as instructed, the presiding juror must date and sign the forms and notify the bailiff. Your decision must be based on your personal evaluation of the evidence presented in the case. Each of you may be asked in open court how you voted on each question.

DISTRICT COURT OF THE STATE OF NITA

FOR THE COUNTY OF DARROW

ROSE HUNTINGTON,
PLAINTIFF

v.

MARK ASTER,
DEFENDANT

Case Number: DC-YR-2-2419CIV

VERDICT

We, the jury, in the above-entitled matter, return the following verdict and each of us concur in this verdict.

I. PROFESSIONAL NEGLIGENCE

We, the jury, find the following:

_____That the defendant, Mark Aster, failed to use reasonable skill and care in drafting the plaintiff's trust.

_____That the defendant, Mark Aster, used reasonable skill and care in drafting the plaintiff's trust.

_____That the defendant, Mark Aster, failed to use reasonable skill and care in carrying out his duties as a trust protector.

_____That the defendant, Mark Aster, used reasonable skill and care in carrying out his duties as a trust protector.

II. BREACH OF FIDUCIARY DUTY

_____That the defendant, Mark Aster, breached the fiduciary duty owed to the plaintiff.

_____That the defendant, Mark Aster, did not breach the fiduciary duty owed to the plaintiff.

III. CONVERSION

_____That the defendant, Mark Aster, transferred funds that constituted an actual and substantial interference with the plaintiff's ownership interest in the property.

_____That the defendant, Mark Aster, did not transfer funds that constituted an actual and substantial interference with the plaintiff's ownership interest in the property.

JURY VERDICT ON DAMAGES

_____General damages are awarded to the plaintiff in the amount of $_____.

[Any additional damage issues are bifurcated for further hearing]

_____General damages are denied to the plaintiff.

____

FOREPERSON

www.ingramcontent.com/pod-product-compliance
Lightning Source LLC
Chambersburg PA
CBHW081126180926
51611CB00004B/63
9781601563347